Brief Dramas for Worship

Brief Dramas for Worship

TWELVE READY-TO-USE SCRIPTS

KAREN FARISH MILLER
and
BRENDA MOTLEY NEWMAN

ABINGDON PRESS / Nashville

BRIEF DRAMAS FOR WORSHIP
Twelve Ready-to-Use Scripts

This book is printed on acid-free paper.

Library of Congress Cataloging-in-Publication Data

Miller, Karen Farish.
  Brief dramas for worship : twelve ready-to-use scripts / Karen Farish Miller, Brenda Motley Newman.
    p. cm.
  Includes bibliographical references.
  ISBN 0-687-03875-8 (binding: adhesive perfect : alk. paper)
  1. Drama in public worship. 2. Christian drama, American. I. Newman, Brenda Motley. II. Title.

BV289.M55 2005
246'.72--dc22

2005011199

05 06 07 08 09 10 11 12 13 14—10 9 8 7 6 5 4 3 2 1
MANUFACTURED IN THE UNITED STATES OF AMERICA

This book is dedicated to
The source of all joy and hope
Jesus Christ
My husband, Perry Miller
My daughter, Elizabeth Miller
My mother and father,
Ruby and Joseph Key Farish
My siblings and their families,
Jessica and Hannah Moffatt
Kent, Sunny, Brian, and Colleen Farish

— Karen Farish Miller

This book is dedicated to
The source of all grace and peace
Jesus Christ
My husband, Don Newman
My sons Alex and Jacob
My mother and father,
Lewis and Ethel Motley
My siblings and their families,
Rose and Dave, Doug and Terri
Ben, Jessica, Stuart, Tyler

—Brenda Motley Newman

Table of Contents

Chapter 1: The Bethlehem Child: Children in Poverty
By Brenda Motley Newman

The Bethlehem child is every child born whose life is full of hardship.
Just as Jesus was born into poverty and violence, modern-day children
cry out as their lives are compromised by hunger and abuse. Use
to raise awareness of programs that serve children in poverty.

Chapter 2: Eli's Wife: A Husband's Tale Brings Hope for Peace
By Brenda Motley Newman

A shepherd's wife ponders the news of Jesus' birth, holding it dear
to her heart. Her feelings shift from fear to expectation and lead finally
to the desire to serve. The theme of peace is highlighted. *The Revised Common
Lectionary*: Christmas Eve (A, B, and C)

Chapter 3: Caroline: A Waitress Receives the Living Water of Acceptance and Hope
By Brenda Motley Newman

A modern-day woman at the well is an exhausted waitress. Poverty and abuse
have colored her life. She meets Jesus on her shift and is touched by his
compassion and upset by his knowledge of her broken life. Acceptance
and hope begin to heal her as a result of the encounter. *The Revised Common
Lectionary*: Year A, Third Sunday in Lent: John 4:5-42

Mary, a sister of Lazarus, grieves for her brother. Her heart is broken and
her trust in Jesus is compromised. Has Jesus abandoned her family?
Mary's hope is restored when Jesus returns and calls Lazarus out
of the tomb. With Jesus' words "Unbind him, and let him go!" Mary's
fear and despair are released as well. Use at any worship service to
assist a church or individual who has experienced crisis, chaos, scandal,
or loss. *The Revised Common Lectionary*: Year A, Fifth Sunday in Lent:
John 11:1-45; Years A, B, and C, Monday of Holy Week: John 12:1-11.

An exhausted Martha puts aside the demands and distractions of life
and experiences Jesus. Explore true perfection, move closer to an
appropriate balance between doing and being, and sit at the feet of
Jesus. *The Revised Common Lectionary*: Year C, Sunday between July 17
and 23: Luke 10:38-42 inclusive; Year B, Fifth Sunday of Easter:
John 15:1-8; Year B, Sixth Sunday of Easter: John 15:9-17.

A businesswoman in ancient Philippi recounts her conversion and baptism
by the apostle Paul. She tells how God's love set people free who were in
various kinds of enslavement. The message of hope and salvation is well suited
for use in a prison, homeless shelter, or any place where hope and recovery
are needed. *The Revised Common Lectionary*: Year C, Sixth Sunday of Easter:
Acts 16:9-15; Year C, Seventh Sunday of Easter: Acts 16:16-34; Year C,
Sunday between June 12 and June 18 inclusive: Galatians 2:15-21

CONTENTS

CONTENTS

She's gorgeous, with her sleek sunglasses and her string bikini,
and King Dave thinks he's in love. He puts out a contract
on her husband, and Bathsheba moves in with him. A storyteller with a
wild circus tale brings King Dave back to reality. King Dave's confession
is a paraphrase of Psalm 51. *The Revised Common Lectionary:*
Year B, Sunday between July 24 and 30 inclusive: 2 Samuel 11:1-15
Year B, Sunday between July 31 and August 6 inclusive: 2 Samuel 11:26-12:13*a*
Year B, Sunday between July 31 and August 6 inclusive: Psalm 51:1-12

When a young Hebrew maiden becomes queen of an empire that
does not worship God, she becomes the only hope of her
people for survival. The impassioned plea from her people to speak
on their behalf moves her to acts of courage and heroism. *The Revised
Common Lectionary:* Year B, Sunday between September 25 and
October 1 inclusive: Esther 7:1-6, 9-10; 9:20-22

Text is NRSV unless otherwise noted.

*Congregation invited to stand.
**The Faith We Sing
***The United Methodist Hymnal
****Draw Me Close: 25 Top Vineyard Worship Songs

Foreword

THERE IS A NEW generation of worshiping people sitting in our sanctuaries every Sunday. They are aware of the tragedies in our world and in their own lives. They are asking hard questions about the purpose and meaning of life. They have come to your church asking if you have answers. And they don't want simple, pat answers.

In this book, Brenda Newman and Karen Miller give you a new way of sharing our Christian faith's responses with these people. These twelve dramas acknowledge real life issues, are faithful to the biblical texts, and offer no simple answers. Instead, they share biblical and historical narratives that enable everyone to identify with these inquirers and catch a glimpse of God's presence with us. As we share these stories together, we are drawn together into a community shaped by God.

These twelve vignettes are rich in possibilities. While all the dramas use women as their central characters, the issues are common to us all. From children in poverty to death in the family to wayward children, Brenda and Karen have addressed the most profound issues of human life. The dramas are linked to *The Revised Common Lectionary*, the Christian Year, prayers and liturgical options, and a host of musical suggestions. The settings may be complex or exceptionally stark. Congregations of any size may use these stories well. The use of these dramas over a period of time will enrich the worship of any congregation.

I encourage you to read aloud, ponder, and offer these stories in your congregation's worship. And then, be quiet, and watch the Holy Spirit work wonders in your midst.

—Andy Langford
Co-Author of *Beginnings: An Introduction to Christian Faith*
General Editor of *The United Methodist Book of Worship*

Introduction

THIS BOOK IS INTENDED for worship leaders, pastors, small group leaders, and others who want to communicate through drama, liturgy, symbols, and silence that Christ is alive, and we can encounter him over and over again. The dramas were not written for scholars, so we have used our imaginations in creating details for some of the stories. We will leave it up to the preachers to bring their best exegetical skills to their sermon preparation. Our hope is to reach hearts and minds by presenting lively characters from the Bible who are not usually in the spotlight.

The resources may be used very simply. Some of the dramas contain descriptions of how to adapt to minimum, medium, or maximum effort, depending on the time and skills of those using the materials. All have been written to be presented using a script. They can be done in reader's theater style, in which the presenter stands at a podium or pulpit and reads, or with the script hidden. Every script offers a suggestion for hiding the script. It will take some rehearsing to be able to read the script with energy and enthusiasm. It is not intended to sound like a lecture! If the script is memorized, it allows the actor to fully engage the audience with both body movements and facial expressions. Even novice performers can aim for this goal, but the main objective is to stimulate creativity in worship.

The acting skills needed are minimal, with the exception of the dialect used in the drama entitled "Mattie May." If untrained persons are using a script for the first time, they should remember to speak very loudly and slowly and yet in a natural way. The dramas are usually short and do not require intricate sets or costumes, although these can add interest if they are used.

To some degree, stage fright can be helpful if it makes us focus and work hard to overcome our natural fear of speaking in front of others. It helps us to remember that we are not just acting a part, we are making an offering of ourselves to God who loves us even if we forget a line or talk too fast. Prayer helps, as does slow, deep breathing. Focus on the theme, not on the audience.

One person can present the drama, though directions are given to show how they can be adapted to more actors. The number of actors available and the needs of the church will determine how the script is used. The dramas were designed for women, but most can be adapted for men.

Aware that churches are using different styles of worship, we have indicated different ways to present the scripts in a variety of services. Some churches use *The Revised Common Lectionary*, suggested scripture readings for a three-year cycle that can be found at Christian bookstores. The readings for each Sunday and holy days are listed for use in a weekly worship service to provide a systematic approach to the use of Scripture.

The lectionary follows the outline of the Christian year. It is a voluntary tool for planning and leading worship and is used by churches of various denominations. We

1

have listed the Sundays that the Scripture passages appear to assist churches that use the lectionary. We have also included a church year listing of the dramas to provide an overview of the year. See Suggestions for Use During the Church Year in the Appendix.

For churches that use contemporary music, we have made some suggestions from recorded and sheet music. Churches with a praise band can add or change the music.

Most of the dramas have options for stage sets, but no sets are required. The dramas differ in length, so we have indicated the presentation time for each one.

In addition to liturgies for worship, we have included a list of possible uses for each script. There are Bible study guides for many of the dramas and two complete retreats. The dramas themselves dictated the type of guides we included. One written to appeal to youth has a youth Bible study. One designed to assist in creating awareness of the needs of children contains specific suggestions about getting involved in helping children. Some of the dramas led naturally to other liturgies, such as Reaffirmation of the Baptismal Covenant and a foot washing. These are included as options.

Our background as United Methodists led us to select the *The United Methodist Hymnal* and *The United Methodist Book of Worship* as resources. The drama about Mary Fletcher represents a piece of Methodist history. Other denominations have resources that can be adapted in place of the suggestions we have given. When possible, we have also used *The Faith We Sing*, an interdenominational songbook.

The Bible is the heart of worship and church life, and we share with worship leaders and pastors the task of finding fresh ways to help people connect the Bible with their lives. These dramas are designed to make this possible. We hope that the Bible characters will provide "ah-ha! moments" when worshipers or listeners enter into the passage in a new way.

When we plan worship, we offer ourselves to God's guidance and pray that God will be glorified. It makes no sense then, if God has done the work, for us to take all of the credit! If an actor did a great job portraying a character from this book or leading a worship liturgy, give praise to God. The goal is to draw people closer to God and to give them a chance for a dramatic encounter.

Worship is fun and creative, whether it is done with a team or alone. It is a joy to find the words, phrases, actions, and themes that let people know they are in God's direct line of vision. We encourage teams of laity and clergy to work together to plan worship and other events in the life of the church. Don't be afraid to offer new ways of allowing God's spirit to minister to people.

Change is difficult for congregations. As trained mediators, the authors have both seen churches in conflict because people have different needs and tastes related to worship. Go slowly with change. Pay attention to resistance and find out what is behind it before proceeding. Care for people more than ideas. However, worship does not need to look and feel the same week after week. Variety keeps it fresh and keeps people on the edge of their seats. Their curiosity will bring them back wondering, "What's going to happen?"

In creating the worship and teaching designs, we have tried to look at what happens in the seasons of church life. What rite of passage is suitable for the parishioner who has suffered a painful divorce, lost an unborn child, said good-bye to a grown child, or learned that he or she has cancer? What is the appropriate experience for individuals and churches who struggle with illness or imprisonment? How do churches celebrate their mission focus? How do women go beyond comfort and find empowerment in their faith? How do we ask God for forgiveness? How do we teach what it means to be "saved"? A church has a life rich with many seasons. God always has something important to communicate, no matter what the season.

These services are designed to connect a human ache with the utterly unfathomable love of God. If they do not fit the circumstances of your congregation, feel free to change them to better serve your purposes. Give special care to express grace and not judgment, to provide hope and not despair.

We hope our ideas will stimulate creativity in others. We would be pleased if those who use this book for worship or other church events would give credit to the publisher, but then use their own creativity to adapt the materials to their own setting. We suggest that those who wish to adapt the pieces in this book consider carefully the power of silence, symbols, and action. Often these have as much or more power than words. Don't be afraid to leave open spaces in which God can interact with people! We've discovered that God can use a grave cloth, a pitcher of water, or a broom to reach people if they are receptive. If the symbols that we've chosen don't speak to you or for you, please select your own.

Thank you for being part of an effort to create places where people make a divine connection. We believe God says "Bravo!" when you invite others to open their hearts for dramatic encounters.

As they say in show business, "Break a leg!"

CHAPTER 1

The Bethlehem Child: Children in Poverty

By Brenda Motley Newman

(Four short monologues that portray the voices of children caught in the cycle of poverty and violence.)

Stage Setting: A large box is placed at the front of the sanctuary. Use microphones for all of the speakers, especially for children and youth. Use the altar table or set up a separate table filled with childhood items. Include items that span from early childhood into the teen years, such as building blocks, stuffed animals, books, balls, a trophy or two, a portable CD player, etc.

Props: Large (refrigerator or dryer) box, bookbags, books, composition books, old robes, blankets, small table with work tools, a piece of cloth, childhood items placed on a central table.

Costume: Speakers wear worn-looking jeans and casual (even torn) shirts.

Presentation: The following speakers take turns using the box: a teenage girl, a teenage boy, two preteen female speakers, and a young boy (not a speaking part) for the four presentations. The reading parts may be presented by one to four readers (preferably older teens or adults).

Presentation time: Fifteen minutes.

Scripts

The Bethlehem Child Theme: (Print this in the bulletin or announce the theme verbally.)

The Bethlehem child is every child born into poverty and violence. It is every child whose life is full of hardship. It is every child who does not receive the basics of food, clothing, and shelter. It is every child who longs for a secure home and who longs for good news. At this season of Advent, we remember that Jesus was born in Bethlehem, into poverty and violence. Throughout the generations, Bethlehem has been filled with all of the reasons God needed to send Jesus into the world—poverty, oppression, abuse, rejection, hatred, and violence. Today, millions long for a secure home, and we all cherish good news.

Monologue 1: *A Teen from Bethlehem: No More Bus Rides*

(Reader states the title as the presenter gets into place. A teenage girl places a bookbag beside her in the box. She pulls a book out of her bag, with the script hidden in the book.)

Teenage Girl: I am supposed to be on the school bus right now, but I can't make myself get on. I don't think Mama will find me here under the back porch. I don't know if you heard the news the other day. Another suicide bomber blew up a bus carrying Israeli school children and commuters in Jerusalem. That was my bus. I wasn't on it that day because I was sick. My best friend died that day. Why was she killed? She never hurt anyone. She was nice to everyone. She was almost the smartest student in the school. *(Open a book or shift position some.)*

Mama didn't make me go to school for two weeks. We cried a lot and went to the services for those who were killed. But now Mama and Papa say we have to go. Why? I don't want to go to school without my best friend. I don't think I can ever ride the bus again. Why should I go to school anyway? If I don't die on the school bus, I'll get blown up while shopping one day, or when I get my first job, or when I am out with friends at a nightclub. My cousin died last year at a nightclub. It was her first trip; she was celebrating her twenty-first birthday. My uncle died two years ago. He was on a bus too. *(Pause a moment.)* I don't think Mama will find me here. I think I'll read for a while.

Reader *(Older teen.)*: The world continues to be devastated by violence and poverty. There are youth, such as those who live in Afghanistan, Bosnia, the Democratic Republic of Congo, Northern Ireland, and on the West Bank and the Gaza Strip, who have known little else but violence. They have personally witnessed the death of too many people. Children who grow up in violence live with fear, depression, and very low expectations for the future.

Youth around the globe have not only witnessed acts of violence but also have become soldiers. Jane Springer, in the book *Listen to Us: The World's Working Children,* dedicates a section to children who work in the military. She notes that children are often kidnapped and forced to become soldiers or join the armies at young ages because their families have been killed, and it is a way to survive. Springer concludes, "If they manage to survive, former child soldiers are often traumatized by the violence they have seen. They may experience nightmares, insomnia (inability to go to sleep), headaches and crying. Other children with brutal war experience become so used to violence that they lose any inhibitions about it and continue to commit violent acts."[1]

There are other equally brutal forms of child labor around the world. Innocence is also stolen from children in the form of child slavery, trafficking, prostitution, and pornography. The Anti-Slavery Society notes that there are an "estimated 200 million child laborers in the world. This is today's world of nine-year-old coal miners and eight-year-old prostitutes and of little girls who work in twelve-hour shifts in sweatshops."[2]

How can the children of the world become compassionate, productive adults when they have known little else but abuse, slavery, and war? How can they dream when they see few jobs waiting for them and danger at every turn?

Monologue 2: *Hiding from Danger: Poverty in the United States*

(Reader states the title as the presenters get into place. An older girl (ten or eleven) and a younger boy are in a large box together, rocking back and forth gently. They are surrounded by old robes and blankets, with the script hidden in a blanket. The girl speaks.)

I think the gunfire has stopped now. But I ain't sure, so we'll stay in the closet a few more minutes. Mama told us every time the shooting starts to crawl quickly from our beds and hide in the closet. If the shooting is outside, we hide in the hallways where there ain't no windows, but if the shooting is in our building, we hide in the closet.

I don't like hiding in the closet because it upsets Jimmie and then his asthma starts. Sometimes I forget to bring his inhaler in the closet with us. I try to remember, but sometimes I forget. But at least the closet is warmer than the hall. We can pull Mama's clothes down around us to keep us warm. I wish there hadn't been no shooting tonight, 'cause now I'm cold and hungry, and I won't get back to sleep. Mama said there wouldn't be no food till lunch. She told us to warm up on coffee and stay under the blankets till she got home. *(Pause.)* We'll stay in the closet a little longer, just in case the gunfire hasn't stopped.

Monologue 3: *Sarah: Longing for a Home*

(Reader states the title as the presenter gets into place. A young teenage girl is in the box when the presentation begins. Hide the script on the front of the bookbag.)

(Gather up books and place them in a bookbag.) I have to hurry up, so I can eat at the shelter and wash up before school. I haven't seen Mama now for two days. She's been gone before. Sometimes she finds work, and we get to stay in a motel. Those are the best times. Then I get to take a hot shower and watch all the television I want. I wonder what it would be like to have a shower and watch TV every night? *(Fold up an old blanket.)* I have to gather all of my stuff now. I hide it in a corner at the shelter. This box may be gone tonight. I think the garbage collectors pick boxes up. *(Pause and put bookbag on shoulder and blanket under arms.)*

My teacher talked about homeless people in class last week. She doesn't know I am homeless. She talked about why people are homeless and how sad it is that homeless children often don't go to college. The hardest things for me are not knowing where I will sleep tonight and not knowing when I will see Mama again. *(Start walking away from the box.)* I have to hurry up because I don't want to be late for school. I don't want to get into trouble because then the school might find out about me. I hope there isn't a long line at the shelter today.

Reader *(Older teen or adult.)*: These are stories of children growing up in poverty in the United States. There continues to be dire poverty across our nation, leaving children in unsafe homes or homeless. In 2000, 11.3% of the population or 3.1 million people lived in poverty. Forty percent of persons living in poverty today are children.[3] Some of these children are being raised in substandard housing with little heat in the winter and infestations of roaches and rats in the summer. They play in streets where violence confronts them in the form of gunfire, drugs, and sexual abuse. In addition to those who live in unsafe neighborhoods, there are the homeless. It is difficult to gather statistics on the homeless because they are often hidden or stay on the move, trying to keep their families together without intervention from the Department of Social Services. The National Coalition for the Homeless notes while there are several national estimates of homelessness, the best approximation is from an Urban Institute study, which states that about 3.5 million people, 1.35 million of them children, are likely to experience homelessness in a given year.[4]

Monologue 4: *Christmas in Bethlehem?*

(Reader states the title as the presenter gets into place. A teenage boy, thirteen or fourteen, is seated at a small workbench with some tools beside the box. The script is hidden among the tools.)

We haven't decorated this year. My family is Christian. Mom made coffee and cookies, but none of our relatives could come because of the curfew. We know there won't be any gifts. Dad hasn't worked in over eight months. I'm older now, but I feel bad for my little sisters. I've been trying to carve them something, but I'm not very good at carving.

(Hold up a tool or piece of wood that has been carved on.) It's been a way to pass the time though. We haven't had many school days. Sometimes, when the curfew is lifted, we will have school for half a day.

Our teacher asked us last week, "Is there still Christmas in this town where Christmas began?" *(Pause. Set down tools or wood and become more reflective.)* I haven't been able to answer her yet. I think she said to write an essay. I guess I'm not very responsible about my homework. It seems like we never turn it in, so I just don't bother with it much.

Is there still Christmas? All I see around me is sadness. The girl next door was killed. Another lady lost her husband. Everybody is poor and afraid. I don't know. Does Christmas come in the middle of wars? It doesn't seem right to me—a God of love in a world of hate. I wonder if God bothers with us any more. Maybe God gave up on us.

I wouldn't say this to Mama or Papa. They pray every day. We have had so many funerals. They say all we have is God. Maybe Mama and Papa are right. When Jesus was born, the world was full of hatred. That's why God sent Jesus. Oh, Jesus, we need you now.

Reader *(Older teen or adult.):* Read Luke 2:1-20.

❋ ❋ ❋

Worship

Worship Bulletin
First Sunday of Advent

Prelude

Bringing Light to the Church

Lighting of the Advent Candles *(Invite children or youth to light the candles each week. Choose siblings, Sunday school classes, or friends.)*

Child 1: Read Isaiah 60:2-3

Child 2 *(Older child.)*: We light this candle as a symbol of Jesus as our Hope. May the lost children of the world know God's living hope. May we bring hope into the lives of God's children this Christmas through offerings and a renewed willingness to reach out to help.

Child 3: Light the first Advent candle.

*Opening Hymns: #211 "O Come, O Come, Emmanuel"***
#428 "For the Healing of the Nations"***

Words of Introduction and Welcome: *(Explain The Bethlehem Child theme.)*

Old Testament Lesson: Isaiah 2:1-5 (This lesson is from Year A of the lectionary. The lessons for the First Sunday of Advent, Years A, B, or C are all appropriate.)

Church Family Concerns

Silent Prayer

Pastoral Prayer

The Lord's Prayer

*Gospel Reading: Matthew 24:36-44 (The lessons for Years A, B, or C are all appropriate.)

Anthem: #2213 "Healer of Our Every Ill"**
(Alternate suggestion: #431 "Let There Be Peace on Earth"***)

Monologue Presentations: (All four readings if used as one service.) "The Bethlehem Child: Children in Poverty"

Responsive Litany: *(Youth or young adult.)*

Leader: I am frightened and cold.
People: I am a child of Bethlehem.
Leader: I am thirsty, hungry, and weak.
People: I am a child of Bethlehem.
Leader: I am an orphan, invisible and alone.
People: I am a child of Bethlehem.
Leader: I am mistreated, neglected, and overlooked.
People: I am a child of Bethlehem.

Leader: I am rejected, tossed aside, forgotten.
People: I am a child of Bethlehem.
Leader: I am afraid to go home.
People: I am a child of Bethlehem.
Leader: I have no home to go to.
People: I am a child of Bethlehem.

Alternate Suggestion for the Responsive Litany: (*Invite four older children or youth to read. Have the readers read from different points in the worship area.*)

Reader 1: I am frightened and cold.
Reader 2: I am a child of Bethlehem.
Reader 3: I am thirsty, hungry, and weak.
Reader 4: I am a child of Bethlehem.
Reader 1: I am an orphan, invisible and alone.
Reader 2: I am a child of Bethlehem.
Reader 3: I am mistreated, neglected, and overlooked.
Reader 4: I am a child of Bethlehem.
Reader 1: I am rejected, tossed aside, forgotten.
Reader 2: I am a child of Bethlehem.
Reader 3: I am afraid to go home.
Reader 4: I am a child of Bethlehem.
Reader 1: I have no home to go to.
All: We are children of Bethlehem.

Offering: Include a special offering for children in poverty.

Children's Choir (*or combined choir or the congregation*): #2193 "Lord, Listen to Your Children Praying" * *

* Doxology: #94 * * *

* Closing Hymn: #206 "I Want to Walk as a Child of the Light" * * *

* Benediction: "**Lord, we are all your children. Come into the brokenness of our world and bless us with your light.**"

***

Weeks 2, 3, and 4

Lighting the Advent Candles

Lighting of the Advent Candles (Week 2): (*Have the acolyte light the first Advent candle when the altar candles are lit.*)

Reader 1: Read Mark 1:4.
Reader 2: We light this candle as a symbol of Jesus as our Way. Many children need a way out of poverty and abuse. May God's Word lead us to help the children of the world. (*Light the second Advent candle.*)

• Lighting of the Advent Candles (Week 3): *(Have the acolyte light the first two Advent candles when the altar candles are lit.)*

Reader 1: Read Isaiah 35:10.
Reader 2: We light this candle as a symbol of Jesus our Joy. May the lost children of the world know God's joy. May we bring joy into the lives of God's children this Christmas. *(Light the third Advent candle.)*

• Lighting of the Advent Candles (Week 4): *(Have the acolyte light the first three Advent candles when the altar candles are lit.)*

Reader 1: Read Isaiah 9:6-7.
Reader 2: We light this candle as a symbol of the Prince of Peace. May the lost children of the world know God's peace. May we bring peace into the lives of God's children this Christmas. *(Light the fourth Advent candle.)*

Prayers and Other Presentations highlighting The Bethlehem Child theme during the Advent Season:

Suggestion 1:

Lord, we pray today for the children of the world.
We pray for those born into poverty.
We pray for those who have been casualties of war.
We pray for those who continue to be scarred by the violence that surrounds them.
Lord, we pray today for the children of the world.
We pray for those who are homeless.
We pray for those who seldom feel safe in their homes.
We pray for the abused and neglected and for those who are tossed aside and rejected.
Lord, we pray today for the children of the world.
We pray for those who are sick and disabled.
We pray for those who are lonely and long for friendship.
We pray for those who have lost a parent.
Lord, we pray today for the children of the world. Amen.

Suggestion 2:

Video:
Children's Defense Fund, "Prayer for Children." Adapted from Ina J. Hughes and narrated by Marian Wright Edelman. Running Time is 2 minutes and 48 seconds. Order: 25 E. Street NW, Washington, D.C. 20001; 202-628-8787.

Suggestion 3:

Marian Wright Edelman's "A Twenty-First Century Prayer for Children." In *Hold My Hands: Prayers for Building a Movement to Leave No Child Behind* (Washington, D.C.: Children's Defense Fund, 2001), 32.

Blessing for Children and Youth

Reader 1: Jesus said: "Truly I tell you, unless you change and become like children, you will never enter the kingdom of heaven. Whoever becomes humble like this child is the greatest in the kingdom of heaven." (Matthew 18:3-4)

"Take care that you do not despise one of these little ones; for, I tell you, in heaven their angels continually see the face of my Father in heaven." (Matthew 18:10)

"So it is not the will of your Father in heaven that one of these little ones should be lost." (Matthew 18:14)

Reader 2: "Jesus said: 'Let the little children come to me, and do not stop them; for it is to such as these that the kingdom of heaven belongs.'" (Matthew 19:14)

Reader 3: "And he took them up in his arms, laid his hands on them, and blessed them." (Mark 10:16)

* Hymn: #2095 "Star-Child" * *

Blessing for the Children and Youth: *(Invite all children and their families to the front of the worship area. If it is a large congregation, rather than moving to the front, invite family members and friends to lay their hands on the children and youth during the responsive litany.)*

Responsive Litany:

All: God of us all, we offer you joyful praise for these children and youth. We praise you as the giver of all life. We come before you with deep thanksgiving for these children and youth, for the joy and hope they have given to us.

Leader: We praise you for the newborns, infants, and toddlers. We praise you for safe deliveries, for the adoption of children and the homes that are welcoming them, and for each of the new and growing families among us. For these, the smallest of our children, we ask for your blessing. Bless their physical, spiritual, emotional, and social growth and development.

People: May God bless you and hold you tenderly.

Leader: We praise you for our preschool children, for their enthusiasm and abundance of energy. We praise you for their constant desire to learn, for their powers of observation and wonder. We thank you for their imagination and appreciation for life. Help us to learn from them. Restore to us the wonder and awe for your creation. Bless these children with health. Protect them from dangers as they rush to discover each new day. Surround them with your constant love.

People: May God bless you and hold you tenderly.

Leader: We praise you for our elementary children. We rejoice at their eagerness to learn and their willingness to serve. In these years of rapid growth and learning, may they receive strong guidance for their faith journeys. May they learn the stories and words from your Holy Word. May they invite you into their hearts and lives and make a commitment to serve you as Lord and Savior. Bless and protect them. Constantly surround them with strong Christian role models. Assure them continually of your love.

People: May God bless you and hold you tenderly.

Leader: We praise you for our middle school youth. During this time of growth and change, help them to begin to discover their many talents and skills. Increase their commitment to follow you and strengthen their faith for the many challenges ahead. Help them when they face negative peer pressure and guide them as they make more and more decisions for themselves. Protect them during these years. Constantly assure them of your presence and steadfast love. Provide them with strong Christian role models.

People: **May God bless you and hold you tenderly.**

Leader: We praise you for our high school youth. We thank you for the many ways they are already serving you in the church and community. We rejoice at those who have made commitments of faith, and we ask that you continue to draw all of the youth close to you. Help them to know how much you love each of them. Develop their talents and skills and guide them into the future you have planned for them. They face daily decisions at school and with their friends. Assist them in these decisions and surround them with strong Christian role models. Protect them on their many adventures. Bless them with wisdom, strength, compassion, and grace.

People: **May God bless you and hold you tenderly.**

Leader: Bless all of the parents of these children and youth. Bless them with health, patience, energy, and wisdom. Increase their commitment to serve you that they may model faith for these children. Bless the new parents among us. Bless those parents who are dealing with a child who is ill. Grant them healing and the constant strength of your presence. For those parents struggling with rebellion, grant them wisdom and daily guidance. Strengthen and give hope to those parents faced with the challenge of disabilities. Surround all of these families with the peace of your continuing presence.

People: **May God bless you and hold you tenderly. Amen.**

Special Music from Choir: #2193 "Lord, Listen to Your Children Praying"**

✳ ✳ ✳

Uses

- **The First Sunday of Advent:** Use the four presentations consecutively. Take up an offering for children in poverty.
  - ❏ *Order of Worship included.*
  - ❏ *Worship suggestions and litanies included.*
  - ❏ *A Blessing for Children and Youth included.*

- **Use as an Advent series:**

  Suggestion 1: (Present the theme weekly.)
  - ❏ First Sunday of Advent: Present the four monologues.
  - ❏ Second and Third Sundays of Advent: Invite speakers from programs that serve children to increase awareness of ways to help. Examples are the Guardian ad Litem program, Big Brothers, Big Sisters program, or Social Services (on the need for more foster homes).
  - ❏ Fourth Sunday of Advent: Have a Blessing for Children and Youth. *(Blessing is included at the end of the chapter.)*
  - ❏ Take up offerings each Sunday for children in poverty, either for the specific program lifted up that week or for one children's cause. Use the litanies and other worship suggestions to highlight the theme each week.

  Suggestion 2:
  - ❏ First Sunday of Advent: Present Monologues 2 and 3 with accompanying readings.
  - ❏ Second and Third Sundays of Advent: Same as in Suggestion 1.
  - ❏ Fourth Sunday of Advent: Present Monologues 1 and 4 with accompanying readings. Have a silent Christmas pageant as Luke 2:1-20 is read. Remove the prop box and replace it with a manger and hay.
  - ❏ Take up offerings each Sunday for children in poverty. Use the litanies and other worship suggestions to highlight the theme each week.
  - ❏ On Christmas Eve or the First Sunday of Christmas: Have a Blessing for Children and Youth. *(Blessing is included.)*

- **Use in Sunday school:**
  - ❏ Invite advocates for children to speak to one large Sunday school gathering on the second and third Sundays of Advent and use suggested worship ideas that highlight the theme for the entire season of Advent.
  - ❏ An adult Sunday school class or small group may also study resources such as:

    The State of America's Children Yearbook, Children's Defense Fund. CDF Publications; PO Box 90500, Washington, D.C. 20090-0500; 202-662-3652.

    Poverty Matters: The Cost of Child Poverty in America, by Arloc Sherman. (Washington, D.C.: Children's Defense Fund, 1997).
  - ❏ A long-term adult study idea: Have a class read and discuss:

    Amazing Grace by Jonathan Kozol. (New York: HarperPerennial, 1996).
  - ❏ A youth Sunday school class may study resources such as:

    Listen to Us: The World's Working Children by Jane Springer. (See endnote 1.)

Stolen Dreams: Portraits of Working Children by David L. Parker with Lee Engfer and Robert Conrow. (Minneapolis: Lerner Publications Co., 1998.)

❏ Have a children's class study missions within your denomination that minister to children in need. Invite them to bring coins to send to one of these ministries.

• **Use on a Children's Sabbath Sunday/Child Advocacy Sunday:** Use Monologues 1, 2, and 3. Take up an offering for a children's cause. Have Sunday school classes participate in studies, such as those suggested previously. Introduce the theme as "May God's Word lead us to help the children of the world."

*Congregation invited to stand.
**The Faith We Sing
***The United Methodist Hymnal
****Draw Me Close: 25 Top Vineyard Worship Songs

1. Jane Springer, *Listen to Us: The World's Working Children* (Toronto, Ontario: Groundwood Books, 1997), 58-60.
2. Anti-Slavery Society, www.anti-slaverysociety.addr.com/clab.htm
3. NCH Fact Sheet #1 The National Coalition for the Homeless, September 2002
4. NCH Fact Sheet #2 The National Coalition for the Homeless, September 2002

CHAPTER 2

Eli's Wife: A Husband's Tale Brings Hope for Peace

By Brenda Motley Newman

Scripture: Luke 2:8-20

Stage Setting: Place a simple wooden chair with a table in front of it at the center of the worship area. Add a piece of pottery and a candle. A bowl containing dough is on the table or the chair.

Props: Chair, table, pottery, candle, bowl, dough, lighter or matches.

Costume: Typical medieval version of biblical clothes. Costumes for traditional Christmas or Easter dramas are suitable.

Presentation: The presenter enters and lights the candle. She then picks up the bowl and begins kneading dough.

Presentation time: Eight to ten minutes.

Script placement: Behind the pottery and other items on the table.

Script

Reader: Read Luke 2:8-20 before the presentation.

Words of Introduction: Enter the home of one of the shepherds privileged to hear the angels' announcement of Jesus' birth. Hear his wife's reflections about the night he came home and told her the news of the Savior's birth. Reflect with her as she ponders the meaning of the Messiah's arrival.

Presenter:

Eli comes home with stories all the time. He and the other shepherds have little else to do sitting out in the fields night after night. Everyone knows they are the best storytellers around. Yet when Eli began to share this tale, a hope deep within my heart began to bubble up. This was real. He had come. Our Savior. And God had announced the Savior's coming to my husband, Eli, first.

Eli had trembled a little when he began to recite the night's events. He ran his fingers through his beard nervously. The night, he said, had been like any other night. Then suddenly, an angel surrounded by a blinding light appeared. His heart pounded. I understood his fear. How he withstood the angel's presence I do not know. I wished once for an angel to appear to me. I wished for an angel to reassure me of the gift of children. We waited five years for Rebecca. The thought frightened me so that I decided I could be content childless before I could face an angel.

Eli hastened to tell me that the angel's first words were "Be not afraid." The angel was a messenger of good news. The good news was the news we had all been waiting for. It had happened in my generation. My grandparents, great-grandparents, and their grandparents before them had waited for the Messiah. Now he had come during my time. I could hardly believe it. It was possible that my daughter might live in a time of peace. I had never felt so alive! I had no idea then, and still months later, have no idea what his birth means. Will we have to wait for him to grow up? Will there be a time of great unrest before he saves us?

I remember the prophet's frightening words: "He was oppressed, and he was afflicted, yet he did not open his mouth, like a lamb that is led to the slaughter" (Isaiah 53:7a). Will the time of peace come in my generation or in my daughter's? I have so many fears. What will be required of us? I have tried to recall all of the scriptures I have heard read in the temple. Most were difficult to understand. As a woman, I am not allowed to study. But I have listened to Eli and my father interpreting them. I have been trying since that joyful night to piece together what is about to happen. Isaiah, the revered prophet, prophesied that the poor would have good news preached to them. Yes, that is why the angel appeared to Eli and the shepherds. *We* will share in God's peace. He is *our* Messiah—the Messiah of the poor, the sick, and the oppressed. *We* will have invitations to his kingdom. He was born in a stable, just like I was. He did not have a fancy birthplace, nor did our little Rebecca. But the angel said more. Eli repeated to me again and again the entirety of the angel's message. "I am bringing you good news of great joy for all the people." I have spent much time pondering on this. This little babe is clearly not only *our* Messiah. He is the Messiah "for all the people." I questioned Eli several times about this portion of the message. He was certain that these were the angel's words, "for all the people." This is the point I have heard so much debate on at the temple. Isaiah referred to this often, yet my people have never completely accepted it. Isaiah prophesied, "And all the ends of the earth shall see the salvation of our God" (Isaiah 52:10b). Many of our people have difficulty believing that God is for everyone. Yet, somehow I have always known it in my heart.

I think it goes back to when I was a little girl. Every year at the Feast of Tabernacles, my cousin Miriam had a way of ruining our joy and unity. Mama said Miriam had a "spirit of discontentment." She could never be happy! I learned then that peace and joy cannot exist for only a few. Those without peace and joy in their hearts will spoil the harmony for the remainder. There cannot be an end to our oppression until the oppressor's hearts are changed also. There cannot be peace on earth until all people know God's peace. The prophet Jeremiah teaches this. Of God's new covenant, Jeremiah wrote: "I will put my law within them, and I will write it on their hearts" (Jeremiah 31:33b).

Eli continued the story excitedly, describing the multitude of the heavenly host who appeared with the angel. He confessed he had been frightened, but with their singing he began to feel expectation. A sense of urgency took over, and he felt a need to see this baby and to share the angel's song. He and the other shepherds made haste to Bethlehem. Eli hesitated at this point. He bowed his head and was silent. I wondered for a moment what was going on. He stammered slowly, "I have never felt so honored, so privileged, so humble. God chose me, a poor, simple shepherd, to tell Joseph and Mary about heaven's visitation announcing the good news concerning their child. I realize that they must have known already, but I was allowed to share the details with them. God loves us. Oh, my heart is so full."

Eli spoke no more that night. We held hands and prayed quietly. I learned later of Eli's glorifying and praising God on the streets of Bethlehem and all the way home. He is such a shy man. He has always told me boisterous tales, but he is known as a quiet man in the village.

I find that my own feelings are constantly shifting from fear to expectation—much like Eli's did that night. All of my people are experiencing a flow of emotions. But we are beginning to understand what will be expected of us. A ceremony included in our Feast of Tabernacles is called the "Illumination of the Temple." We send out such a blaze of light that all of Jerusalem witnesses it. Isaiah said that we are to be a light to the nations. This baby, our Savior, will fill our hearts with peace and goodwill. And we will spread that peace and goodwill until the whole world knows God's goodness. This is how I will serve my Lord. *(Speaker stands during this last paragraph and begins lighting candles. At Christmas Eve, a candlelight service follows. Light a Christ candle at a Sunday morning service. Light a Christ candle and an array of candles at a contemporary service.)*

Worship

Worship Bulletin
Christmas Eve

Prelude

Bringing Light to the Church

Responsive Call to Worship:

> Leader: In that region there were shepherds living in the fields, keeping watch over their flock by night.
> **People: Then an angel of the Lord stood before them, and the glory of the Lord shone around them, and they were terrified.**
> Leader: But the angel said to them, "Do not be afraid; for see—I am bringing you good news of great joy for all the people:
> **All: To you is born this day in the city of David a Savior, who is the Messiah, the Lord."** (Luke 2:8-11)

*Hymn: #236 "While Shepherds Watched Their Flocks"***

Words of Welcome

Old Testament Readings on Peace (Invite three lay people from three generations to read.)

> Isaiah 2:1-5 Isaiah 9:2-7 Isaiah 11:1-10

Call to Prayer: As we hear these visions of peace and long for their fulfillment, let us pray for our broken world:

Leader: Lord, how we long for a world that does not learn war anymore, where the wolf dwells with the lamb, and the Prince of Peace rules.

People: Come into the brokenness of the world, Lord.

Leader: Lord, we lift up the leaders of the world. May they open their spirits to the leading of your Spirit. We ask that you raise up mature, spiritual leaders who know you and will work for the welfare of all people.

People: Come into the brokenness of the world, Lord.

Leader: Lord, we lift up the people who are caught up in the cycle of poverty, oppression, and violence. We lift up those who live in fear each and every day, who do not have enough food for their families, and who have experienced more abuse than respect.

People: Come into the brokenness of the world, Lord.

Leader: Lord, we pray for mediators and peacemakers. We ask that you sharpen their skills, bless their work, and increase their numbers.

People: Come into the brokenness of the world, Lord.

Leader: Lord, we have heard the good news from the angels. We have heard the good news from your Holy Word. We have heard the good news from your Spirit. We pray for those who have not heard the good news. Send them to us and us to them.

All: We rejoice that the Prince of Peace has come and is with us. Help us, Lord, to share your great joy with ALL the people.

Praise Reports: We are here tonight to celebrate the good news of Christ the Lord, and his presence with us. I invite you to share your joys, offers of praise, and good news at this time.

Children's Choir: #228 "He is Born"***
                     #217 "Away in a Manger"***
                     #238 Hymn of Praise: "Angels We Have Heard on High"***
                     (or #2232 "Come Now, O Prince of Peace"**)

Children's Moment
  Suggestion: Share the following story.

"Good News"
By Brenda Motley Newman

"Mama, come quickly!" Scott shouted, as he raced up the driveway. Scott's closely cropped hair kept his curls from bouncing, but nothing could have kept his excitement from showing. "Mama, I found Pinstripe! Mama, I found Pinstripe!"

Scott's mom opened the screen door and reassured her son, "I'm coming in just a second."

Pinstripe had been missing for three days. It is not unusual for cats to wander off now and again, but Pinstripe had always stayed close to home. Scott pulled his mom along as if Pinstripe's life depended on their immediate attention.

"Oh, they are precious!" Scott's mom exclaimed almost in a whisper. The five tiny balls of fur were nestled against their mother, nursing. None of them slightly resembled the mom's black and white markings. They were shades of yellow and gray, though the runt of the litter was charcoal black.

"Mama, we have to call Daddy and Grandma and Steve! Can Steve come over and see them? Can I go tell Mrs. Brown? They are behind her garage, and I bet she doesn't even know about them. And I want to tell Michael and Tyler." The pitch of Scott's voice became higher as he continued to list his friends and neighbors. His mom tried to calm him down, but then they both hurried back to the house to start calling Scott's dad and grandma.

Mrs. Brown peeked out of her front door, and Scott and his mom waved their arms, "We have kittens! We have five kittens!"

Say: Scott was really excited about the kittens. Have you ever had good news that you wanted to share with everyone? I want to share another story with you about good news. *(Read the story of the angels' visit to the shepherds from a children's Bible.)* The shepherds received good news on the night that Jesus was born, and they were so excited that they told everyone about it. That is what Jesus wants us to do today. We don't have to run up and down the streets, but Jesus wants us to let everybody know that he is here and that he loves us all. *(Hand each child an unsigned Christmas card and ask each to share the good news by sending the card. Close with a thanksgiving prayer.)*

Gospel Reading: Luke 2:8-20

Words of Introduction

Monologue: "Eli's Wife: A Husband's Tale Brings Hope for Peace"

Candlelighting Ceremony: *(The performer lights a candle from the Christ candle and then lights the candles of the ushers, who proceed to light the candles of the worshipers sitting at the end of each pew. The light is then passed across each pew. Have someone turn off the lights as soon as the performer's candle is lit.* It is important to have "fire marshals" prepared in case of fire. Volunteers are fine but do seek anyone with experience in fire fighting to serve in this capacity.)

*Hymn: #239 "Silent Night, Holy Night"***
(The hymn is begun as soon as the head ushers' candles are lit. The congregation continues to sing until all candles are lit.)

*Benediction: **"Fill our hearts with peace and goodwill, Lord. And strengthen us to spread your peace and goodwill until the whole world knows your salvation."**

* * *

Sunday Morning Service

Use the same service. Close with the lighting of the Christ candle or a special arrangement of candles. #251 "Go, Tell it on the Mountain"*** is an appropriate closing hymn.

Alternate Worship Outline

Use PowerPoint® for songs, responsive prayers, the Lord's Prayer.

Worship Set including Christmas Music (Church Praise Band)

Praise songs:
#15 "Come Now Is the Time to Worship"****

#50 "Isn't He"****

#2096 "Rise Up, Shepherd, and Follow"**

Opening from the Children:
Reader 1: "But the angel said to them, 'Do not be afraid; for see—I am bringing you good news of great joy for all the people: to you is born this day in the city of David a Savior, who is the Messiah, the Lord.'" (Luke 2:10-11)

Reader 2: "This will be a sign for you: you will find a child wrapped in bands of cloth and lying in a manger." (Luke 2:12)

Reader 3: "And suddenly there was with the angel a multitude of the heavenly host praising God and saying, 'Glory to God in the highest heaven, and on earth peace among those whom he favors!'" (Luke 2:13-14)

Children's Choir: #228 "He is Born"***

Words of Welcome and Announcements

Praise Reports *(Invite the congregation to share good news received during the week.)*

Prayer and Lord's Prayer

Children's Moment *(See Christmas Eve Service.)*

Worship Set 2 (Church Praise Band—Praise selections.)

Old Testament Readings on Peace: *(See Christmas Eve Service.)*
(Video Suggestion: Display a video of alternating war scenes and peaceful scenes during the readings on peace. Use appropriate background music.)

Call to Prayer *(See Christmas Eve service.)*

Gospel Reading: Luke 2:8-20

Words of Introduction

Monologue *(Close with the lighting of the Christ candle and/or an array of candles.)*

Offering:
Worship Special: #2097 "One Holy Night in Bethlehem"**

* Hymn: #251 "Go, Tell it on the Mountain"***

* Benediction *(See Christmas Eve service.)*

***

Bible Study on Peace

(Start with the discussion questions if used after the worship service or use as below.)

- Share prayer concerns and offer an opening prayer.
- Invite participants to share any "peace-filled moments" they experienced during the week.
- Scripture Lesson: Luke 2:8-20

Words of Introduction

Monologue Performance: "Eli's Wife: A Husband's Tale Brings Hope for Peace"

Discussion Questions

1. One of the first thoughts the wife had as she heard the story of Jesus' birth from her shepherd husband was, *"It was possible that my daughter might live in a time of peace."* The Israelite people had been taught the words of the prophets from the Old Testament, and this vision of peace was deeply entwined with the coming of the Messiah. Read Isaiah 2:4*b*.

> *"They shall beat their swords into plowshares*
> *and their spears into pruning hooks;*
> *nation shall not lift up sword against nation,*
> *neither shall they learn war any more."*

The reading of this powerful vision creates a deep longing for peace. **Say:** Put into your own words your vision of peace for the world, your community, your church, and finally, your family.

2. The words from Isaiah 2 are inscribed on the United Nations Headquarters in New York City, across town from the former location of the World Trade Center. **Ask:** What is an appropriate response to this vision of peace when we often feel forced into situations of conflict, as is the case with terrorism?

3. We recognize the loss of human life because of conflict and the dangers associated with conflict. Ronald S. Kraybill in *Peace Skills: Manual for Community Mediators* writes:

> One reason conflict is so dangerous is that human beings have invested lavishly in one particular response to it: the technology and applications of violence. Everyone knows that to prevail in war, it is necessary to invest in weapons and train vigorously in their use. Most nations spend more money on "national defense" than on education, health care, and all other human services combined. Military academies abound, but what about people and places equipped to assist in peaceful resolution of conflicts? How many people do you know who have invested so much as an hour of conscious effort in learning skills for constructive, nonviolent ways of responding to conflict? If we pray and prepare for the use of violence, we will reap violence. If we want peace, we must begin to practice and prepare in the arts of peace.[1]

Increasingly, communities are offering mediation centers or dispute settlement centers to solve disputes in businesses and families, and courts are encouraging the use of mediation. **Ask:** Have you experienced a formal mediation process in your work setting or in any other setting? If so, are you willing to share both the experience and the outcome of this intervention? *(In your response, it is important to honor confidentiality.)*

Can you recall a time in the past year when you sowed discord? *(Ask the question and invite the group into a time of silent prayer. Encourage participants to seek forgiveness and to lift up current conflicts burdening their hearts.)*

What have you done in the past year to bring peace into the lives of people around you? *(Ask this question and invite the group to continue in silent prayer. Encourage participants to offer thanks for peaceful resolutions.)*

Challenge the group to explore opportunities to learn mediation and peacemaking skills. Contact your local mediation center and ask if they offer workshops. Training opportunities are also available from:

JUSTPEACE Center for Mediation and Conflict Transformation
100 Maryland Ave. NE
Washington, D.C. 20002
(202) 488-5647
Fax: (202) 488-5639
justpeace@justpeaceumc.org

Lombard Mennonite Peace Center
101 W. 22nd St. Suite 206
Lombard, Ill. 60148
(630) 627-0507
Fax: (630) 627-0519

4. The shepherd's wife shared her childhood learning that "Peace and joy cannot exist for only a few. Those without peace and joy in their heart will spoil the harmony for the remainder. There cannot be an end to our oppression until the oppressor's hearts are changed also. There cannot be peace on earth until all people know God's peace." *(Share a simple time when another person's misery ruined an outing.)* **Say:** Consider the violence in society and its root of injustice and misery. Connect some recent news events with the statement from the shepherd's wife. *(Discuss whether that event would have occurred if the offender had known justice and mercy in his/her own life).* **Ask:** How is your peace and joy disrupted by the injustices of the world?

5. We are called to be more than peace lovers; we are called to be peacemakers or peace builders. The shepherd's wife pondered the meaning of Jesus' birth and wondered when the time of peace would come. She also asked, *"What will be required of us?"* **Ask:** What current activities does your church engage in that promote justice and work toward peace? *(Brainstorm new ideas. Write these ideas on a poster or large sheet of paper and present them at an upcoming church board or mission meeting.)*

6. Read Isaiah 9:2-7 as the closing Scripture. Repeat verse 6:

> *"For a child has been born for us, a son given to us;*
> *authority rests upon his shoulders;*
> *and he is named*
> *Wonderful Counselor, Mighty God, Everlasting Father, Prince of Peace."*

Jesus' title "Prince of Peace" continues to stir up the longing for peace in each of us. It also challenges us to be witnesses to God's peace. The shepherd's wife decided that her call was to spread the message of peace and goodwill until the whole world knows God's goodness. **Let us spend a moment in silent prayer and discernment as we consider God's call to share his vision of peace and to become skilled peacemakers in the world.**

✳ ✳ ✳

Uses

- Christmas Eve service: Use as the sermon for the Christmas Eve service, with the candlelighting ceremony immediately after the presentation. *Christmas Eve Order of Worship included.*
- Contemporary service: *Worship outline included.*
- Advent services: Use on a Sunday morning during Advent.
- Advent Bible study: Use as a lead-in for a study on peace. *Study guide included.*

The Revised Common Lectionary
   (Years A, B, and C) Christmas Eve

*Congregation invited to stand.
**The Faith We Sing
***The United Methodist Hymnal
****Draw Me Close: 25 Top Vineyard Worship Songs

---

1. Ronald S. Kraybill, *Peace Skills: Manual for Community Mediators* (San Francisco: Jossey-Bass Inc., 2001), 3-4.

CHAPTER 3

Caroline: A Waitress Receives the Living Water of Acceptance and Hope

By Brenda Motley Newman

Scripture: John 4:5-42

Stage Setting: Place a round or square table with a salt and pepper shaker on it at the front. An optional idea is to add several identical tables with salt and pepper shakers to lend the feel of a restaurant. When used in conjunction with a Service of Congregational Reaffirmation of the Baptismal Covenant, a round table is best. Add to your prop list from four to six buckets of water and a large cross. Hide the buckets and cross under the table. The cross will be the table centerpiece, so be certain that it can be seen over the buckets.

Props: Table, salt and pepper shakers, menu, rag, pitcher of water, glass.

Costume: An apron with white or light-colored clothing underneath and hair net (optional).

Presentation: The presenter wipes off a table, sits down, picks up a menu, and begins speaking.

Presentation time: Six to eight minutes.

Script placement: In the menu.

Production options:

Minimal effort: Present as above with one speaker who reads from the script hidden in the menu.

Medium effort: Using gestures and facial expressions, presenters pantomime the roles of Jesus, the boss, and the waitress while one reader stands at a podium or pulpit and reads the script.

Stage setting: Place four tables on the stage area. One table is in the corner with stacks of papers. One table is at the other end with pitchers of water and stacks of glasses. Two tables are in the center, set with salt and pepper shakers.

Props: Four tables, two sets of salt and pepper shakers, pitchers of water, stacks of glasses, stack of papers, menus, pad and pencil, unlit cigarette, ashtray, rag.

Costume: Jesus–golf shirt and khaki-colored pants; Boss–large apron; Caroline–as noted above.

Script

Caroline: I'm not even sure what time it was when he walked through the doors. The hours blur together when you work fourteen-hour days. I know the lunch crowd had gone, my feet were aching, and my back had the dull nagging throb that is my constant companion. *(Stretch and hold lower back.)* The other waitresses were giggling at a corner table, glancing up now and then. They gather there every day between the lunch and dinner shifts. I'm not welcome at the gossip table. My occasional black eye and the unpleasant visits from my boyfriends exclude me from their circle. I see them making the same mistakes I have made. But who am I to give advice?

He caught my attention when he came in. I know all of the regulars, and most new guys wear factory logos or nametags on their shirts. I went over to take his order, and asked him, "Do you know what you want?"

He asked for a glass of water and then said gently, "Do you know what *you* want?" I'd had enough of smart-alecky jerks, so I left before I said something rude. *(Pause and pour a glass of water.)*

When I came back with his water, he persisted, "Do you know what you want? If you knew the gift of God, and who it is that is saying to you 'Give me a drink,' you would have asked him and he would have given you living water."

As tired as I was, this fella didn't sound like he was jerking me around. His eyes were so penetrating that I began to feel uncomfortable. "Sir, if you have water, why did you come in here asking me for some? What is this living water?" *(Periodically twists the glass of water or even drinks a sip.)*

He told me that everyone who drinks of this water he has will never thirst again. We get a lot of freaks and fanatics, and I couldn't decide about him. I couldn't help but ask him for some of this living water. His eyes seemed to bore a hole through me and he said to me, "Go, call your husband and come here."

I got scared then. My heart started beating real hard. "I don't have a husband."

Then he said to me, "You are right, for you have had many men, and each of your children has a different father."

I remember leaning on the table for support. I thought I was gonna faint. What does this guy want from me? Is he from Social Services? I work hard to take care of my kids. I'm not no perfect mom, but I take care of my kids.

The boss musta noticed my leaning, because he yelled at me, "Hey, Caroline, are you okay?"

The stranger reached out and softly touched my hand, "It's okay, Caroline. I'm here because God loves you."

I couldn't figure it all out, "You offered me a gift from God, living water. What church are you from?"

His voice was firm, "Woman, what matters most is not which church you attend, but that you worship God in truth."

Something deep inside of me was stirring. I'd had enough of hypocrites and church. I'd had enough of being treated like a third-class citizen. But the emptiness and weariness of my spirit suddenly wanted to grasp every word this man was saying. I wanted this living water. I said, "I know that when Jesus comes back, he'll know who really worships God."

He said to me then, "I am he."

The tears streamed down my face, and he wiped them all off. I felt the deep hurt in my soul and the weariness in my body begin to heal. For the first time since I was a young waitress sitting at the corner table looking desperately for someone to really love me, I felt hope. Maybe Grandma was right when she took me to Sunday school week after week. "Jesus loves you, Caroline," she told me every week, "Jesus is gonna come back some day, and we won't be poor no more. He loves all of us." I had been too tired, too beat down to hear my soul crying out.

Could this mysterious, gentle stranger have been Jesus? To be honest, I don't know. But I go with my kids to Sunday school every week. I pray again. I'm not living with a man anymore. I still work here every day. But my life is not the same. God came and gave me what I most needed—acceptance and a reason to hope again.

***

Worship

Worship Bulletin
Third Sunday in Lent

Prelude

Bringing Light to the Church

Responsive Call to Worship:

Leader: We have come to the well today, Lord.
People: Some of us are thirsty and tired. We long for your living water.
Leader: We have come to the well today, Lord.
People: Sometimes we feel like outcasts. We feel diminished and dismissed. We long for your acceptance.
Leader: We have come to the well today, Lord.
People: Some of us feel beat down and put down. Restore our hope.
Leader: We come to the well today, Lord.
All: Meet us at the well, Lord, with your living water. Meet us at the well, Lord, with acceptance and hope.

* Hymn: #352 "It's Me, It's Me, O Lord" ***

Opening Prayer: "O God, we come during this season in Lent. By your redeeming power, create in us clean hearts and put within us a new spirit. Surround us with mercy and assure us of your love. In Jesus' name we pray. Amen."

Words of Welcome

Praise Reports and Testimonies

Children's Choir: #273 "Jesus' Hands Were Kind Hands"***
                 #191 "Jesus Loves Me"***
                 #156 Hymn of Praise: "I Love to Tell the Story"***

Church Family Concerns

Silent Prayer

Pastoral Prayer

The Lord's Prayer

Offering

   Special Music: #2104 "An Outcast among Outcasts"**

*Doxology: #94***

Children's Moment
   Suggestion: *(Bring small paper cups and a pitcher of water. Start by pouring each child a small cup of water. Invite the children to share all the ways they have used water during the past week. (Bathing, drinking, swimming, fishing, washing dishes, washing clothes.) Then stress the importance of water. Water is so important to our bodies that we can live only one week without it. Eighty percent of the earth's surface is water.)* **Share:** We are studying a story this morning about a woman at a well. In olden days, you had to walk to a well every day to get water. *(You may want to bring a picture of a well.)* The buckets were heavy, and sometimes it was a long trip. *(Another idea is to bring a bucket of water and let each child attempt to lift it.)* A woman went to a well one day and Jesus was there. Jesus told her he could give her living water, and she would never thirst again. The woman didn't really understand, but Jesus was telling her that he was the Savior, that he gives all of us life. After they talked some more, she believed that Jesus was the Son of God, and then she went and told others. Jesus wants to give all of us living water. That means that Jesus loves us and gives us water and all we need for life. *(An added suggestion is to find tiny buckets at a discount store and give each child a bucket as a reminder that God always has water for us and will help us when we need and ask.)*

Gospel Reading: John 4:5-42

Monologue Performance: "Caroline: A Waitress Receives the Living Water of Acceptance and Hope"

Special Music: #394 "Something Beautiful"***

(Brief Meditation or Time of Prayer Is Appropriate)

Closing Hymn: #122 "God of the Sparrow God of the Whale"***

*Bringing Light to the World

*Benediction: **"May you hear your soul crying out for God. May you drink the living water Jesus is holding out to you."**

Worship

Worship Bulletin
Baptism of the Lord Sunday

Prelude

Bringing Light to the Church

Responsive Litany:

Leader: We have come to the well today, Lord.
People: Some of us are thirsty and tired. We long for your living water.
Leader: We have come to the well today, Lord.
People: Sometimes we feel like outcasts, rejected and forgotten. We long for acceptance.
Leader: We have come to the well today, Lord.
People: Worries and concerns overwhelm us at times. We long for good news.
Leader: We have come to the well today, Lord.
All: Meet us at the well, Lord, with your living water. Meet us at the well, Lord, with your words of life.

* Opening Hymn: #600 "Wonderful Words of Life"***

Words of Welcome

Old Testament Reading: Isaiah 43:1-7

Special Music: #2218 "You Are Mine"**

Praise Reports and Testimonies

Children's Choir: #277 "Tell Me the Stories of Jesus"***

* Praise Hymn: #2006 "Lord God, Almighty"**

Church Family Concerns

Silent Prayer

Pastoral Prayer

The Lord's Prayer

Offering

Special Music: #2104 "An Outcast among Outcasts"**

* Doxology: #94***

Children's Moment
   Suggestion: *(Bring a bucket of water and invite each child to lift the bucket.)* **Share:** We are reading two stories about water this morning. The first story is about Jesus' baptism. *(Read the story from any children's Bible.)* Jesus was very special to God. God let us know that Jesus was God's Son when he was baptized. When people are baptized it is very special. It is a way of saying you believe that Jesus is God's Son and loved you by dying on the cross for your sin. We are all special to God. The

Bible teaches this in another story about water. This story tells about a woman who went to a well and met Jesus. Jesus told her he could give her living water. She believed Jesus was the Son of God and that he loved her. Jesus gives us water and all the things we need. *(An added suggestion is to find tiny buckets at a discount store and give one to each child as a reminder that God always has water for us and will help us when we need God most.)*

Gospel Reading: John 4:5-42

Monologue Performance: "Caroline: A Waitress Receives the Living Water of Acceptance and Hope"

(Ushers come forward after the presentation and transform the dining table to a "well" with buckets of water placed around the table and a cross in the center. A soloist or the choir sings #394 "Something Beautiful" during this transition.)

A Service of Congregational Reaffirmation of the Baptismal Covenant *(See pp. 111-114 of The United Methodist Book of Worship or The United Methodist Hymnal, pp. 50-53.)*

The congregation is invited to come forward and touch the water in the buckets. The choir may sing softly. Appropriate songs include #2132 "You Who are Thirsty,"** #488 "Jesus, Remember Me," *** and #357 "Just as I Am, Without One Plea."****

* Closing Hymn: #604 "Praise and Thanksgiving Be to God"***

* Benediction: **"May you hear your soul crying out to God. May you drink the living water Jesus is holding out to you."**

Alternate Worship Outline

Worship Set: *(Open with a worship set by praise band.)*
  Suggestions:
  #2 "Arms of Love"****
  #15 "Come Now Is the Time to Worship"****
  #20 "Cry of My Heart"****

Words of Welcome and Announcements

Responsive Litany: *(See Responsive Litany in Baptism of the Lord, Order of Worship. Display on PowerPoint® or overhead projection.)*

Praise Reports and Testimonies

Prayer and Lord's Prayer *(Display Lord's Prayer on PowerPoint® or overhead projection.)*

Children's Moment
  (See suggestion from Baptism of the Lord, Order of Worship.)

Reading: John 4:5-42 *(Have three readers: a narrator, Jesus, the woman. This simple dramatic reading adds emphasis to the conversation between Jesus and the woman.)* Added suggestion is to display a PowerPoint® presentation of mission trips, tired workers, people in the shadows of life, etc. Use an opening and closing slide of an old well. Appropriate background music: #488 "Jesus, Remember Me"*** and #357 "Just as I Am, Without One Plea*** or #2104 "An Outcast among Outcasts"**

Monologue Performance: *(Waitress takes off her apron and takes items off the table at the end. Put the cross in the center of the table and the buckets around the cross. The praise band may play softly or the solo #394 "Something Beautiful"*** may be sung.)*

A Service of Congregational Reaffirmation of the Baptismal Covenant follows. *(See The United Methodist Book of Worship, pp. 111-114. Invite the congregation to come forward and touch the water. Show the responses of the service on a PowerPoint® screen, overhead projector, or printed bulletin. Background music is appropriate. See earlier suggestions.)*

Closing Music: #600 "Wonderful Words of Life"***

Benediction: *(See suggestion from Baptism of the Lord, Order of Worship.)*

* * *

Adult Bible Study

(Start with the discussion questions if used after the worship service or use as below.)

Open the lesson with prayer.

Read John 4:5-42.

Present the script.

Discussion Questions:
1. In this encounter, Jesus plowed through a series of obstacles that often stand in the way when we are called to witness. The first obstacle is prejudice. Jesus challenged both the prejudice between the Jews and Samaritans and the discrimination against females that restricted contact between males and females. **Ask:** What are some of the prejudices Jesus might challenge today? What do you think is the root of prejudice? *(Fear, a view of the world that there is not enough for everyone.)* How would you explain the fear behind prejudice? What are ways you see this fear driving nations apart today? What are ways you see this fear being acted out in your own church or community?
2. The disciples were led out of their comfort zones in Jesus' encounter with this woman. **Ask:** What activities have you participated in recently that were out of your comfort zone? Share both personal adventures and ways you have reached out for Christ. What ministry has your church engaged in during the past year that was out of its comfort zone?
3. The waitress in the monologue had become cynical about the church. **Ask:** Can you remember a time when you felt cynical about the church? What encouraged you to attend church when you were cynical? What led you to attend today? What can you do to reach individuals who have become cynical about the church? How can the church address those who are disillusioned with their faith and organized religion?

4. The waitress was familiar with rejection. Many individuals have experienced rejection at one time or another. Each time we are hurt or feel like a third class citizen, there is the tendency for a part of us to harden. We trust less, and we tend to isolate ourselves even further. **Ask:** Can you think back to one or more of these times in your life? If you feel able, share how you responded. Can you recall a time when you may have caused another to feel undervalued or treated another with little respect? What do you think were the consequences of your actions for the individual and for yourself?

5. Review verses 27-42 of John 4. The Samaritan woman becomes a powerful witness as the result of her encounter with Jesus. **Ask:** What do you think made her such a powerful witness? How can you become a more powerful witness? *(List the obstacles Jesus overcame such as prejudice, cynicism, and the desire to stay in our comfort zones. Brainstorm ideas to help Christians overcome such obstacles.)*

Close with prayer.

***

Uses

• Traditional or contemporary worship: Use during the season of Lent, or as a prelude to a Congregational Reaffirmation of the Baptismal Covenant.
   Third Sunday in Lent: *Order of Worship included.*
   Baptism of the Lord Sunday: *Order of Worship included.*
   Contemporary worship: *Worship Outline included.*
• Evangelism program: Use as a lead-in at a lesson on reaching those outside the church.
• Adult Bible study: *Guide included.*

The Revised Common Lectionary
   Year A, Third Sunday in Lent: John 4:5-42

*Congregation invited to stand.
**The Faith We Sing
***The United Methodist Hymnal
****Draw Me Close: 25 Top Vineyard Worship Books

CHAPTER 4

Mary: Daring to Hope Again

By Karen Farish Miller

Scripture: John 11:1-7, 17-44, 12:1-8

Costume
  Minimal effort: Everyday clothing.
  Medium effort: A long dress or tunic, with a shawl or scarf over her head.
Props: Rumpled strips of muslin cloth. Two-inch squares of the same cloth, each
  with a small safety pin attached. One for every person attending worship.
Setting: None required.
Presentation time:
  Part 1: Two minutes
  Part 2: One minute
  Part 3: One minute
Script placement: Hidden behind the cloth.

Scripts

Part 1

(Mary enters with rumpled muslin cloth in her hands and stands center stage or at the pulpit.) My brother Lazarus came from the market telling us about this man he'd met named Jesus. Jesus had touched a leper and healed him! We'd heard about him before, how he ate in the homes of outcasts and sinners. My sister Martha and I couldn't wait for him to come to Bethany.

When he arrived, I stopped everything. I sat at his feet and soaked in everything he had to say. I had much to learn, and he had much to teach me. When he spoke, it seemed God was with us and we were blessed.

I can't yet believe what happened later. Our brother Lazarus became ill. Through the long hours that followed, Martha and I talked about the miracles we had heard that Jesus performed. We thought if we sent him word that Lazarus was sick, he would come and make him well. Everything would return to normal. So we sent for Jesus to come. We waited and waited, but Lazarus slipped away. My heart was broken. Martha was inconsolable. Nothing returned to normal.

I remember thinking that Jesus didn't care, or he would have come when we asked him. I was engulfed in a dark sea of loneliness and despair. We were all shaken to the core.

I had a thousand unanswered questions. Had Jesus abandoned me? How could I ever trust Jesus again? Did he even know I was suffering? Was anything he taught us, anything we believed, really true? What were we to believe now? Everything had changed.

We watched and wept as they put Lazarus in the tomb. Four days after he died we heard that Jesus was coming, but by then it was too late. Martha said he was calling for me, so I ran to where he was and knelt at his feet. I said what was on my heart, "Lord, if you had been here, my brother wouldn't have died." I wept. Jesus wept with me. I was baptized with his tears.

Part 2

(Holding the cloth for everyone to see.) Do you see this cloth? Do you know what it is? It's proof that God is still in control, even when everything seems to be spinning out of control. That's what we thought, those who watched Lazarus die.

Jesus came to the cave where Lazarus was buried. He was very sad. He told the men to take away the stone. He looked up to heaven and said a prayer, then he shouted, "Lazarus, come out!"

Lazarus came out with his hands and feet bound with these strips of cloth. Jesus said, "Unbind him, and let him go!"

Lazarus and I have spoken many times about what happened to him. I wanted to know what it was like to be dead and come back. He doesn't know anything more about it than we do.

Once I saw him sitting by the entrance to the cave that had been his tomb. I sat down quietly beside him. He said, "I thought there was no escaping death, no way out, and no bridge back. I don't know why Jesus brought me back. I don't understand it. But if he can bring me back from the dead, nothing can stand in his way. He is stronger than death, stronger than anything. He is the Messiah of God!" We sat there a long time, pondering this great mystery.

I kept the grave cloth to remind me of Jesus, the one who changed everything.

Part 3

Six days before Passover, Jesus came to our home. Martha served him dinner at our table, and Lazarus ate with him. As I looked at Jesus sitting there beside Lazarus, my precious brother, my heart was overwhelmed with love for him. I wanted to bathe him in my love. I took a pound of perfume made of pure nard and poured it on his feet. I wiped his feet with my hair, and the house was filled with the fragrance of the perfume.

One of the disciples complained that it was a waste of money. But this was about my love for him and preparing him for whatever was coming next in his life. His extravagant love was poured out when he unbound Lazarus. Now it was time for me to pour out my love on Jesus.

❋ ❋ ❋

Worship

Worship Notes: The service draws together a community of compassion to affirm God in the midst of the pain of life. In preparation for the service, participants can be encouraged to bring with them symbols of the things they are grieving that they are ready to give to God's care. These may be items they have loved or despised. Some may wish to put items in a shoebox and tape the box closed so that no one else knows what they brought.

Worship Bulletin
Order of Worship

Lighting of Candles

Greeting and Introduction: *(Describe the experience that has caused the church to come together as the community of compassion at this time.)* **Say:** Each of us has choices about how we will respond to events in our lives that cause us grief. We can become hard, bitter, and angry. Another alternative for us is to allow difficulties to open us to God's healing in new ways. By reaching out to God, we can grow deeper in our faith and our trust.

If we allow our hearts to become poisoned, we put ourselves on the casualty list. When we choose trust and faith over fear and doubt, we will find hope that will carry us through.

I invite you to come apart for a while to be with Jesus. Allow yourself to see his face covered with tears as he sat with those who were filled with dark despair. Allow Jesus to touch you with his healing love, so you might find resurrection and hope.

Opening Prayer (All Pray)
Humble Jesus, draw close to us. Our hearts have been weighed down with suffering. We have found it difficult to be thankful these days. We find it easier to dwell in hopelessness and despair. We long to be able to feel and pray a real prayer of gratitude. We ask for the grace to find that gratitude in our hearts. Sometimes we remember your goodness toward us and feel thankful. Other times, we want to shout out our pain to you. There are even times when we feel we can't call out to you. We wonder if you care about us at all. We pray that you will accept us as we are, for we long for your love to renew us and give us hope. In the name of Christ we pray. Amen.

Music: *(Select one of the following.)*
#2136 "Out of the Depths"**
#2169 "God, How Can We Forgive"**
#2171 "Make Me A Channel of Your Peace"**
#534 "Be Still, My Soul"***

Monologue: Part 1 "Mary: Daring to Hope Again"

Silence

Scripture: Matthew 5:3-11

Litany

Leader: When darkness fills our lives, we wonder, "Where are you, Jesus? Do you even care about us?"

People: Jesus is doing the same thing today as on the day he went to the tomb of his friend Lazarus—weeping for us and drying our tears.

Leader: We feel lost and alone. Sometimes we feel like we don't know who we are.

People: When we remember the suffering Christ and the despair and sorrow of his friends and followers, we know that we are not alone. Many have walked this way before.

Leader: It has seemed unbearable at times to endure our losses and experience our pain.

People: Christ assures us that he is patiently waiting with us as we endure distress. Our trials are not overwhelming to him.

All: Thanks be to God and to our suffering servant Jesus Christ. We open ourselves to you now, so you may create life out of death, carve hope out of despair, and restore our wholeness. Amen.

Monologue: Part 2 "Mary: Daring to Hope Again"

Silence

Scripture: Ecclesiastes 3:1-8

Message: *(Suggested titles: "The Mystery of Suffering," "God's Great Recycling Plan," "All Our Sins and Griefs to Bear," "Resurrection Faith")*[1]

Response to the Word *(Optional.)*: In the raising of Lazarus from the dead, Jesus said, "Unbind him, and let him go." There is much that binds us. *(Use this list or make your own.)*

- Resentment
- Sadness
- Anger
- Feelings of betrayal
- Depression
- Loneliness
- Fear

We cannot give up some of these feelings until we have decided that we no longer want them to be a part of our lives. And even then, we cannot overcome them entirely on our own. We need the strength of God and the caring community to help us let go of the things that bind us.

Some of us are prepared for this to be a time of letting go, in order that we might have a new, fresh beginning. Others are here for other reasons. Some are here mainly to support others, to be the witnesses to the acts of courage that are going to be made here today.

Prior to this service, you were invited to bring an object or items that symbolized something you have been grieving, so that you can give it to the care of Christ. You were invited to bring it in whatever form you wished. Now is the time to decide if you are ready to release this burden totally to Jesus. There is no pressure for you to do anything that you are not ready to do. On the other hand, sometimes we need to have a set time when we tell ourselves, "I'll let go of it then. I'll quit worrying about it at this hour of the day." For some of you, this is that moment. We are sorrowful that you had to carry this burden and are praying for you as you release it.

As we enter into this sacred time, I invite you to think about the history of what you are giving up to Christ today. You may close your eyes if it will help you to

CHAPTER 5

Martha: Prescription for Peace

By Karen Farish Miller

Scripture: Luke 10:38-42 or John 15:1-11

Stage setting: No set required. If scenery is used, the set is made to look like a home.
Props: A broom on the floor in the middle of the stage and a table and chair.
Costume: Apron over a simple tunic. Martha's hair is unkempt and she has perspiration across her forehead.
Presentation time: Two to three minutes.
Script placement: On the table.

Script

(Martha walks slowly to the center of the stage area, pushes her hair out of her face and speaks slowly.) Yesterday my sister Mary and I heard that Jesus and his friends were coming to our village today. We were eager for him to come to our home, so we began to cook and tidy up. Mary and I worked side by side all day long. When they arrived in town, I welcomed them and invited them inside.

That's when I saw them. Cobwebs in the corners of the room. *(Hands on hips.)* Sweeping the cobwebs was Mary's job! They were hanging there in full view. Anyone who saw them would think I was too lazy to sweep them away. *(She scowls and picks up a broom that has been left on the floor.)* I left to put out the meal, and Mary came into the room where they were sitting. She sat down quietly near Jesus. I kept waiting for her to help me, but she just sat there!

(Martha turns the broom so the straw is facing her and the handle faces the ground. She gives a disgusted look to the motionless broom.) I wove my way through the crowd with my arms piled high with sleeping mats. One of the men reached out his arms and said, "Here, let me help you with those."

I shot a glance at Mary sitting motionlessly at Jesus' feet *(She looks at the motionless broom again and makes an angry face.)* and said, "No, no, of course not. You go on with your visit." Then I left. Mary was not moving a muscle. *(She turns the broom right side up.)*

Finally I couldn't stand it any longer. I went to Jesus *(She holds the broom by the handle with one hand, elbow straight, and acts like she is talking impatiently to the broom.)* and said, "Lord, don't you even care that my sister has left me to do all this work by myself? *(She points her finger at the broom.)* Tell her to help me."

He looked into my eyes and said, "Martha, you are so anxious and troubled." Well, I had every right to be worried! He looked over at Mary and back at me. "Martha, your joy is gone. Mary has chosen the good portion."

(With the broom in both hands, she holds it parallel to the floor and looks at it.) I looked back at Mary sitting at his feet, worshiping him, adoring him. I realized why she was getting the attention that I craved as a reward for my work. Jesus didn't care whether the house was clean or the meal prepared; he cared about us. Mary received his love. I let the demands of the house organize my life and block Jesus out. I thought my worth depended on my work.

(She puts the broom on the floor and sits quietly at the chair next to a table.) I had only let Jesus into my house. I needed to be still and listen so that I could let him into my soul. *(She folds her hands and bows her head.)*

Worship

Worship Outline
(Adaptable to Traditional, Contemporary,
Blended, or Praise Worship.)

Welcome and Announcements

Introduction: Every broadcast of the children's television program Mister Rogers' Neighborhood began the same way. Mister Rogers came in the door, greeted the audience, took off his jacket, and put on a sweater and sneakers. He would sing, "Won't You Be My Neighbor?" and would invite children to be a neighbor in a wonderfully imaginative and safe neighborhood. Mister Rogers signaled to children that there was a time to leave the cares of the world behind and be present in a playful universe.[1]

As we grow from children to adults, life brings new demands and responsibilities. We can get tied up in doing well in our work, creating the perfect image, and getting all the pieces of our lives right. It is easy to put aside the need to play, giggle, and enjoy our neighbors. We can neglect the development of honest human relationships, as well as our relationship with God. We feel we must pretend that our lives are perfect, so no one will guess that we are really flawed beings.

One of the reasons that Mister Rogers appeals to adults as well as children is his philosophy of life, which is found in his book, *The World According to Mister Rogers*. He wrote, "Some days, doing 'the best we can' may still fall short of what we would like to be able to do, but life isn't perfect—on any front—and doing what we can with what we have is the most we should expect of ourselves or anyone else."[2]

The unholy quest for perfection can make us burned out and exhausted. We can even resent those who are able to truly enjoy life. The thing that is missing in this scenario is deep fellowship with Jesus Christ. The prescription for inner peace is to regularly spend time resting with the Savior and abiding in his love.

In these moments of worship today, we want to grow closer to God. Let us allow God to remove anything that keeps us from being fully open to Christ and our neighbors. Let us allow God to transform and use all that is within us to God's glory. May we find deep, spiritual rest in God.

Music:
#2128 "Come and Find the Quiet Center"**
#2215 "Cares Chorus"**

Prayer:
We open ourselves to you, O God. If it is your desire that we move about in haste and accomplish much, we beckon you to provide the motivation and energy. If you want us to slow down, Lord, teach us how to pace ourselves. If you want us to sit still, teach us how to quiet our spirits and simply be. Quiet the voices within us that drive us to do and to be more than is humanly possible. In the name of Christ, save us from ourselves. Amen.

Children's Moment
(Can be used with or without the book listed here.) **Say:** We talk on the phone to our friends. Can we talk to God on the phone? How do we talk with God? Jesus talked with God and taught his followers to talk with God. Where can we go that God will not hear our prayers? Listen to this story that will help us understand. **Read:** *Can I Pray With My Eyes Open* by Susan Taylor Brown.[3]

Special Music: "Oh Lord, You're Beautiful"[4]

Monologue: "Martha, Prescription for Peace"

Music: *(Choose from the songs listed below.)*
#47 "In the Secret (I Want to Know You)"****
#61 "Lord Reign In Me"****
#66 "More Love More Power"****

#133 "Leaning on the Everlasting Arms"***
#130 "God Will Take Care of You"***
#382 "Have Thine Own Way, Lord"***

Scripture: Luke 10:38-42 or John 15:1-11 *(Additional scripture reference: Psalm 46:10.)*

Message: *(Possible titles: "Doing Versus Being," "How To Get Fired Up, Not Burned Out," "The Myth of Perfection," "Be Still and Know")*

Response to the Word: *(Guided Visualization Experience.)*

Say: Sit comfortably with both feet on the floor and your hands resting in your lap or on your knees. Close your eyes. Imagine you can isolate the most critical, perfectionist part within yourself. This part of yourself has a voice. What does this voice sound like? Is it clear and loud? Is it soft and mysterious? Is it harsh and demanding? What does it sound like to you?

What does this voice say to you? Perhaps it says something like this, "If you try hard enough and follow all of the rules, everything will go as you planned, and everyone will love you and you'll feel good all of the time." Perhaps it says, "Don't try that. You will make a fool of yourself." Maybe it says, "If you can't do something well, don't do it at all."

Imagine sitting at the feet of Jesus with a backpack on your back. You can see his face and look into his eyes. You can see his hands and the garment he is wearing. You sit there and Jesus begins to speak to you. He begins by saying, "You have many heavy things in your backpack. Let me carry those for you." You remove your backpack and you realize that it is filled with heavy stones.

You remove the first stone. You can feel the weight of it in your hands. You think about what it stands for and why you feel you must carry it. Jesus reaches out his hand and you put the stone into his palm. He places it in his backpack. The next stone you hand him is something else heavy that you have been carrying. You put it into Jesus' outstretched hands. You continue stone by stone, large and small, picking them up, remembering what they stand for, and handing them over to Jesus.

When you have lifted all of the large stones, there are still some small stones in the backpack. These are anxieties and worries that keep you from feeling free. You hand these over to Jesus until your backpack is completely empty. You place the pack on your back. You feel light, almost weightless.

Jesus looks you straight in the eyes and says, "There is need of only one thing." *(Pause.)* He hands you something. What does he give you?

You realize you feel so loved and accepted that the critical perfectionist is struck mute. The power that has driven your perfectionist self is transformed by a new source of positive energy. You are released from the fear of not being perfect. There is new energy entering your mind, body, and spirit. The perfectionist self is powerless to drive you.

Tell yourself that whenever you feel the critical, destructive power returning, you can return to the feet of Jesus. All you need to do is become very still and quiet and bask in the love of one who understands you completely. Take a few moments to finish the experience at the feet of Jesus. You feel lighter, yet full of all the good that Christ has for you. When you are ready, open your eyes.

The critical self can convince us that we have the possibility of a flawless existence. But this paralyzes us and makes us ashamed when we fail to live up to the high standards we set for ourselves. We are better served by acknowledging that we can never be perfect, no matter how hard we try. True perfection can be found in God. Only God is worthy of our adoration and praise. At any moment, we can sit at the feet of Jesus and worship in our hearts.

Music:
#2070 "He is Exalted"**
#2086 "Open Our Eyes"**
#2087 "We Will Glorify the King of Kings"**
#2088 "Lord, I Lift Your Name on High"**

* Benediction: #477 in *The United Methodist Hymnal* "**Open wide the window of our spirits, O Lord, and fill us full of light; open wide the door of our hearts, that we may receive and entertain thee with all our powers of adoration and love. Amen.**"

* Choral Benediction: #143 "On Eagle's Wings"***

※ ※ ※

Adult Bible Study

Words of Introduction: Jesus and his disciples went to the home of two sisters, Mary and Martha. The visit evoked very different responses from the sisters. Listen for these differences so we can talk about them after the presentation.

Monologue presentation. "Martha: Prescription for Peace"

Discussion Questions. Eugene Peterson paraphrases Jesus' words to Martha this way, "Martha, dear Martha, you're fussing far too much and getting yourself worked up over nothing. One thing only is essential, and Mary has chosen it—it's the main course, and won't be taken from her" *(The Message)*. The Bible study will focus on what Peterson calls the "main course," and the *New Revised Standard Version* calls the "better part."

1. Read Luke 10:38-42 aloud.
2. On a white board or large sheet of paper, list words that describe the response of the two women to their guests.
3. Martha, who was working hard to create a place where Jesus would feel at home, began to resent Mary because she didn't share her worries or the workload. She was getting the attention that Martha craved, without doing anything. Martha approached Jesus, interrupting him with her concern. What did she demand of him? Did he do what she asked?
4. Based on their actions, what did Mary and Martha feel is essential?
5. Read aloud John 15:4-11. What did Jesus mean when he used the word "abide"? Contrast what happens when someone abides in him and what happens when one does not abide in him.
6. Read aloud John 12:3-8. Judas rebuked Mary for anointing Jesus' feet with costly perfume and wiping them with her hair. When Judas suggested that the money spent on perfume would better benefit the poor, Jesus responded that she was preparing him for burial. He indicates that the poor will always need help, but that "you do not always have me." What do you think Jesus meant?

Life Application

1. What did Jesus object to in Luke 10:41? *(Fretful worry, distractions that keep his followers from resting in him.)* Describe how your life reflects this.
2. What actions did Jesus praise? *(Being still, listening, and anointing his feet with oil.)* Describe how your life reflects this.
3. Does Jesus object to work or servanthood? *(No, there is a time for everything.)*
4. Are you more like Mary or Martha?
5. How do you interpret John 12:8 when Jesus indicated there would always be the need to minister to the poor, but there is also a time to rest in his presence? *(He acknowledged that he would not always be physically present to his people, and they needed to use the time he was with them to have fellowship with him. There is a time to do and a time to be. Both are important.)*
6. List some ways to rest in the Lord or become renewed spiritually. *(Pray, meditate, listen to Christian music, be silent, walk on the beach, walk a labyrinth, pray with a friend, meditate on an icon or other Christian art, create a piece of artwork, read or listen to a favorite Christian book, talk to a mentor or friend, write in a journal, attend a worship service, attend a silent retreat, seek spiritual guidance or spiritual direction.)*[5] Make a plan to spend some time in spiritual rest in one of these ways in the next three days.
7. Discuss with a partner how you will provide time for this without making it another task to accomplish. The purpose is rest and renewal.

Closing: #607 "A Covenant Prayer in the Wesleyan Tradition" *The United Methodist Hymnal*

***

Uses
- Any style of congregational worship: *Outline included.*
- Retreat or spiritual renewal event: *Guided Visualization included.*
- Adult Bible study or small group: *Guide included.*
- Use script to narrate a liturgical dance by Mary and Martha.
- Combine chapters 4 and 5 for A Women's Spiritual Enrichment Retreat called "Sisters in Christ" focusing on the characters of Mary and Martha.

The Revised Common Lectionary
    Year C, Sunday between July 17 and 23 inclusive: Luke 10:38-42
    Year B, Fifth Sunday of Easter: John 15:1-8
    Year B, Sixth Sunday of Easter: John 15:9-17

*Congregation invited to stand.
**The Faith We Sing
***The United Methodist Hymnal
****Draw Me Close: 25 Top Vineyard Worship Songs

---

1. The segment of *Mister Rogers' Neighborhood* in which Fred Rogers enters his television house and changes into his sneakers and a sweater is found on either of the following, which may be ordered as VHS or DVDs: "Adventures in Friendship" or "A Day at the Circus." They are available through the online catalog of Family Communications, Inc. at http://www.fci.org/shopping/default./asp. Both were published in April 2005 by Anchor Bay Entertainment and directed by Hugh Martin III and David F. Chen. If a children's program is provided during this worship service, they can view the video, then discuss with their leader the way Mister Rogers helps them accept themselves, like Jesus did.
2. Fred Rogers, *The World According to Mister Rogers* (New York: Hyperion Books, 2003), 14. Family Communications, Inc. is donating the profits from this book to The Fred Rogers Fund, which will continue his work promoting healthy emotional, social, and intellectual development of children.
3. Susan Taylor Brown, *Can I Pray With My Eyes Open* (Winnipeg, Manitoba, Canada: Hyperion Books for Children, 1999).
4. "Oh Lord, You're Beautiful," *WOW Worship Yellow 2003 Songbook*. Franklin, Tenn.: Brentwood-Benson Music Publishing, Inc., 2003. Also available on CD.
5. To explore spiritual practices, read Corrine Ware, *Saint Benedict on the Freeway: A Rule of Life for the 21st Century* (Nashville: Abingdon Press, 2001). There is a helpful study guide at the back of the book.

Lydia: A Witness to the Power of Christ to Open Hearts, Open Minds, and Open Doors

By Karen Farish Miller

Scripture: Acts 16:11-40, Galatians 2:19-20

Production options:

> **Minimum effort:** Everyday clothing.
>
> **Medium effort:** Lydia in a long tunic or robe and hair in a bun. She enters with a large piece of purple fabric, unfolds the fabric, drapes it gracefully across the altar, podium, or pulpit and puts her script on top of it and begins reading. Use the script below, eliminating all suggestions for other characters.
>
> **Maximum effort:** The narration is done by Lydia or by someone offstage using a microphone. Pantomime actions. The name of the drama is on an overhead projection.

Cast:

Lydia: Hippie who wears a flowing purple skirt, tank top, sandals. Her hair is in dreadlocks or is a bright color.

Sarida: Preppie who wears a short skirt, tight shirt, straight or crimped hair.

Paul: Outsider who wears a plain button-down shirt and pants that do not sag.

Jailer: Jock who wears a football jersey with shoulder pads, jeans.

Slave owners: Two skateboarders wear black T-shirts, baggy shorts, caps on backwards or knitted caps. Can carry or ride on skateboard.

Stage setting: A fishbowl filled with water and clear marbles sits on an altar or table to the left of the stage area. On the right is a jail cell.

Production time:

> Shorter version: Two minutes
> Longer version: Five minutes

Script placement: In the Bible.

Script

Lydia: (*Lydia enters with a Bible and a piece of purple fabric. She unfolds the fabric, drapes it gracefully across the altar, podium, or pulpit and puts down the Bible.*) My name is Lydia. My home was one of the first places Christians gathered to worship. *(She picks up a Bible and opens it. She reads from the script for the rest of the monologue.)* You can read about me in Acts 16 in your Bible, but I want to tell you in my own words about God's mighty work in Macedonia, a Roman province in Europe.

One day I went down to the river with some of my friends to pray. Some travelers came along, Jews from Tarsus. *(Paul enters.)* The one named Paul talked with us about Jesus. We were praying to God, but we didn't know Jesus was God's Son. *(Paul pantomimes as if he is telling about Jesus.)* Paul proved this by sharing his teachings and his healings. He told us that Jesus was executed on a cross *(Paul extends his arms.)* as a sacrifice for sin and that God had raised him from the dead. *(Paul raises his hands and looks up.)*

We were all astounded by what he said. I asked Paul how he could be certain this was true. *(Lydia lifts her palms to Paul.)* He said that after Jesus came back from the dead, he appeared to him in a flash of light! *(Paul puts his hands over his eyes.)* Paul said that he had been a miserable man, torturing people who followed Jesus. He said the risen Christ had struck him blind to get his attention. *(Paul removes his hands and extends them, as if he cannot see.)*

Then when Paul was convinced that Jesus was Lord, he confessed his sins. *(Paul kneels down and lifts his eyes toward the ceiling, putting his hands together to pray.)* Jesus forgave him and gave him a new life. *(Paul stands up tall and smiles, putting his hands out toward Lydia.)* He said that God's love was so great for us that God gave his very own Son to save us from our sins.

Paul said that we could have a relationship with this risen Christ. He invited us to make Jesus the Lord of our lives right then. *(Paul nods.)* The more he spoke, the more I felt compelled *(Lydia smiles at Paul and nods her head, taking his hand in hers.)* to open my heart to what he told us. I wanted to know Jesus as my Lord and be washed clean of my sins. I wanted to feel that enormous love of God that Paul felt. I understood that sin must be awful if it took the death of a human being to bring relief from it.

(Lydia goes to the pulpit or podium where the purple cloth is.) I had been a businesswoman for many years, selling purple cloth. *(She lifts up the cloth on the altar, podium, or pulpit.)* I made the cloth for the chief priests' robes and for other wealthy and powerful people. But I had never heard anyone as powerful and convincing as Paul.

(She kneels down.) I accepted Jesus as my Lord and was baptized in the river that very day! *(Paul puts his hands on her head. She stands, smiling broadly, hugs Paul gently, and spins around.)*

I've thought a lot about the day I was baptized. In making purple cloth, the fibers of wool and flax are placed in a vat with beautiful violet dye. The fabric enters the vat one color and comes out entirely different. *(She motions as if she is putting cloth in the vat and taking it out.)* That process is very similar to what happened to me the day I was baptized in the river. That day I was immersed in love and forgiveness, and I came out entirely different. *(She puts her hand on her chest.)*

When I came out of the water the love of the Savior saturated every fiber of my being. *(She moves her hands from her head to her shoulders as if she is dropping water on herself.)* I felt perfectly loved and accepted. It was so powerful that I wanted other people to experience that saving love of God.

(For a short version of the drama, end here.)

Paul and the other disciples were traveling from place to place to share this good news. They didn't have a place to stay in Philippi, so I invited them to stay with my family. When my family members and others in our community heard the message of God's Son, they were changed and gave their lives to Jesus, just as I did.

(Sarida enters, followed by the slave owners.) One who was changed was Sarida, a servant girl I had seen when I was in the market selling cloth. She was making a lot of money for her owners *(She has wads of money in her hands, and the slave owners force her to give it to them.)* by telling the future. *(Paul walks over to her.)* When Paul and his friends came to the market, she followed them everywhere they went. Over and over she kept saying, *(Sarida raises her hands in a frenzied motion.)* "These men are slaves of the Most High God."

After several days of this, Paul said to the spirit that possessed her, "Come out of her in the name of Jesus." *(Paul touches her gently on the shoulder with one hand.)* All at once, the spirit was gone. *(Sarida suddenly stands up straight, smiles, straightens her clothes.)* She became calm and filled with joy. She completely lost the ability to tell the future.

(Slave owners raise a clenched fist and look threateningly at Paul.) The men who owned Sarida got very angry at Paul. Sarida had been quite profitable for her masters. *(The slave owners chase Paul and grab his hands, dragging him toward the jail. Pantomime a beating, with Paul falling down and covering his face with his hands facing the slave owners.)* They beat Paul and his friend Silas with rods. *(Slave owners exit.)*

Our hearts were broken when we witnessed these faith-filled men being beaten in the market. They were arrested and put into prison. *(Jailer puts Paul in jail.)* We were frightened for them and for ourselves. But Paul wasn't afraid. Although he was bruised and covered with gashes, Paul was praying and singing in jail. *(Paul pantomimes lifting his head and praying.)*

(In a hushed voice.) That night there was an earthquake, which shook the jail and opened the doors to the cells. *(Paul moves around as if the jail is shaking. The jailer enters.)* The jailer thought his prisoners had escaped. If they had, he knew he would be punished mercilessly. *(Jailer looks around, but he can't see anything.)* He believed it would be easier to take his own life than face torture, so he pulled out his sword and prepared to thrust it into his chest. *(Jailer draws a sword and puts it to his chest.)*

When Paul and Silas saw what the jailer was trying to do, Paul pleaded with him, *(Paul kneels on one knee.)* "Don't take your life. Give it to Jesus. Put your trust in him. Then you'll live as you were meant to live."

The jailer couldn't believe this strange turn of events. *(Jailer puts sword a few inches away from his chest, then a few more, and finally puts his sword away.)* As he spoke with Paul, the jailer's despair turned to joy. *(Paul puts his hands on the shoulders of the jailer, then the jailer kneels, and Paul puts his hand on his head as if baptizing him.)* He was converted and baptized. *(Jailer and Paul exit, both smiling.)* He went home and told everyone what had happened. His entire family was converted right then, in the middle of the night. There was a big celebration.

The Roman officials did not know Paul was a Roman citizen, or they would never have punished him without a trial. When Paul told the officials that he was a citizen of the Roman empire, they apologized and let him go. Then he and Silas came to my home one last time before they left Philippi.

God's power is stronger than anything I have ever known. It can overcome slavery of any kind. It can free persons from fear, death, depression, and sadness. God's power gives hope and life. It is the power of God through Jesus Christ. It has made me a new person in Christ.

Worship

Worship Bulletin
Contemporary Worship Outline

Welcome and Announcements

Praise songs:
  #79 "The Lord Almighty Reigns"****
  #72 "Show Your Power"****
  #76 "Take My Life"****

Greetings

Prayer

Drama: "Lydia: A Witness to the Power of God to Open Hearts, Open Minds, and Open Doors"

Offering
  Special Music: "Love Came Down" by Lindell Cooley.[1]

Scriptures: Acts 16:11-40, Galatians 2:19-20

Message: "Dyed in the Wool Conversion," "How to Make God Happy"
  United Methodists adopted the phrase, "Open hearts. Open minds. Open doors. The People of the United Methodist Church" as part of the denomination's media campaign created by Igniting Ministry at United Methodist Communications. To create a sermon that goes along with this theme entitled, "The Power of God to Open Hearts, Open Minds, and Open Doors," tell how God opened the hearts of Lydia and the jailer and his family, how God opened the mind of the demon-possessed slave girl and the officials who finally released Paul, and how God opened the doors of the jail cell and released everyone from some kind of imprisonment. Demonstrate how God is still opening hearts, minds, and doors today.

Worship Songs:
  #2108 "O How He Loves You and Me"**
  #2137 "Would I Have Answered When You Called"**

Closing: Invite the participants to come to the fishbowl, put their hands in the water, and take with them a sign of God's love and a reminder of the power of God to open hearts, minds, and doors. *(They each take a clear marble from the bottom of the fishbowl.)*

* Benediction: #2281 "May You Run and Not Be Weary"**

Youth or Seeker Bible Study

1. Watch a video clip about people being saved from drowning: (Obtain any necessary permissions.)

Simon Birch[2]—Simon and his friends were returning home from camp. The bus driver veered off the road to avoid hitting a deer and watch what happened. (The bus lands in a lake and all of the children are frightened. Simon and his best friend save everyone on the bus, but Simon is pulled under with the bus. He eventually comes to the surface, where he is rescued.) Start when the bus goes over the bridge and end when the children are rescued and the last ones are walking up the hill.

2. Talking Points:

There are many ways to talk about the beginning of a relationship with Jesus Christ. One that you have probably heard is "getting saved." In the video, the characters are about to drown and someone must save them. We are going to see a drama based on a passage from Acts 16:11-40. Let's listen and watch for the ways that people were saved.

3. Present drama

4. On white board or large sheet of paper list the people who were saved in some way.

   A. Lydia and her family: from sin to salvation
   B. Sarida: from a life of slavery
   C. Paul: from imprisonment
   D. Jailer: from suicide

5. **Ask:** Has anyone here ever been saved from drowning? *(Draw parallels between being saved from drowning and saved from sin.)*

6. Guided Imagery Prayer

Lord God, we are caught in a riptide that drags us far from the shelter of your shore. We are pulled, invisibly, by the desire to make ourselves into something you never intended us to be.

At first it felt like an adventure when we sloshed out toward the distant horizon. Yet the waves pounded us mercilessly, and we knew we were in danger. The currents that took us out to sea will never bring us back to you. We are lost and adrift.

Some of us have lost our sense of direction, and we don't know which way to swim, even if we had the strength to battle the undertow. Our eyes scan the surface of the water for shark fins, jellyfish bubbles, waves that would push us under and hold us down. We drift along, uncertain of whether there is hope of returning to shore.

Between the breakers we can see the lifeguard stand, just a speck on that broad beach. Someone is standing there. Is it someone strong enough to save us? We cry out with a watery voice, "Help!" We wonder if the person can hear us.

"Relax," shouts the voice, "I'm coming to rescue you." What a helpless feeling to have to be saved. We want to fight! Surely we can make it on our own. We try one last time to swim with all our might, but our spirits are exhausted from trying to cross the current and our bodies are no match for the power of the ocean.

We must be saved by power beyond our control. We must be brought to the beach by one who is stronger than we are, one who knows the terror of the tides, one who can carry not only his own weight but also our own.

We make out the outline of broad shoulders flinging arms into the water. Strapped to his body are grace and hope in the form of a bright orange life belt. Huge waves wash over us as we wait. Our eyes burn with salt and tears as we ponder how we got to this place. We swam out farther than we should have, and though we knew the tides could be strong here, we thought we were stronger.

He said to relax. We stop fighting against the tide. No more flailing of legs and arms. When we let go, the tide's power seems to lessen. We are lifted and surrounded by life saving grace, orange, buoyant, keeping our heads above water. The lifeguard clings tightly to us as he slowly swims to shore. Flat out on the sand we get a look at his face and realize he is familiar to us.

Wasn't he the Christ who was tossed about and saved so many years ago? If he had died then, at the mercy of the waves, we might also have perished here. Because he was saved, we are saved. Breath becomes regular again, heart rate returns to normal, but we are changed forever.

O God of grace and hope who preserves our lives, your saving love is more abundant than the grains of sand. Thank you that we are not at the mercy of the tides but saved to live again. In the name of Christ our Life Savior. Amen.

Music: Play the music or sing the song "Dive"[3] about taking a risk and diving into God.

Adult Study
A Witness or a Wanna Be?

Present the drama. Introduce the study by talking about the impact that Paul and Lydia had on the people of their day because of their witness. Contrast what it means today to be a Witness or a Wanna Be. Make a handout of the following outline by leaving blank where the words are in bold. Participants can fill it in during the presentation.

1. Wanna Be's are not totally convinced that bringing new people to Christ is **urgent** or **essential.** They may say they believe it is important, even read books to help become more effective in it, but they do not do it. Witnesses are totally and utterly committed to **bringing new people to Christ.**
2. Wanna Be's don't seek out or spend time with people who are not Christians or who are not in the church. It forces them out of their **comfort zone.** Witnesses spend time with people outside of church potluck suppers or Sunday school. They **build relationships** so that they can share their faith.
3. Wanna Be's think of themselves as **church members or pastors.** They spend their time with people who are already converted. Witnesses consider themselves **home missionaries.** They **invite, convert, and disciple.** They reach people outside the church.
4. Wanna Be's fear that they don't have the **time or resources** to bring people to Christ and disciple them. They **procrastinate,** so they don't get around to reaching out to people who need Christ. Witnesses believe that God is abundantly gracious in all ways and that **every need will be provided.** They are waiting and ready for someone to provide an opening to serve **him or her or to talk about Christ.**
5. Wanna Be's are **afraid.** They fear failure, rejection, and feeling uncomfortable. They are afraid that they don't know what to say or do to bring someone to Christ. Witnesses develop their **skills** and **confidence** so that nothing will hold them back.

6. Quick-fix, shallow images of **evangelism** make Wanna Be's shy away from talking to people about Christ. Witnesses learn about sharing their faith with **integrity** and accept that people are likely to have mixed reactions. They also know that **discipling** takes time and patience.

7. Bringing people to a saving relationship with Jesus Christ requires more **authenticity, intimacy, and interpersonal skills** than Wanna Be's feel comfortable sharing. Talking about personal faith or praying for others is an **intimate** experience. Some are not willing to become vulnerable with family or friends, much less with people who do not know Christ. Witnesses are not afraid to get involved with other's people "stuff," their **sin** or their **temptation.** They are committed to **caring,** no matter what.

8. Wanna Be's **are intimidated** by the value systems of other people. Even though their commitment to Christ may run deep, they feel that if they share their values with others, they might offend them. Witnesses are willing to do **whatever it takes** to bring people to Christ and are especially sensitive to those who have a different set of values.

9. Wanna Be's have **"spiritual amnesia."** They have become hurt, jaded, or numb and can't remember the joy of their salvation. They can't share it with others because it is not real. Witnesses **get help** if there is something that keeps them from growing, including deep grief and loss, serious illness, marriage breakdown or divorce, depression, church conflict, or addiction. They do not let anything steal the **peace that passes all understanding.**

10. Wanna Be's are **pew warmers** and they have a take-it-or-leave-it attitude about being in worship. They complain about the color of the carpet or who is going to be the acolyte. Witnesses are **hungry** to be with other Christians, to hear the gospel proclaimed, and to worship Christ. They **prepare** their hearts for worship, bring their Bibles, and feast on the Word of God. They get fueled up to have the energy to witness for Christ.

How can we become Witnesses instead of Wanna Be's?

1. The power to become a witness is not from us, but from the **Holy Spirit!** Read 2 Timothy 1:7-13 and Acts 1:8. God did not give a spirit of timidity (some versions say cowardice or fear), but the spirit of power, love, and self-control.

2. We can be transformed by **the renewing of our minds!** Read Romans 12:1-2. We can learn how to share interpersonally the things that are in our heart and experience.

3. When you bring someone to Christ, you make God **ecstatic!** Read Luke 15:10. Don't you want to be responsible for a party in heaven? Pleasing God is what life is all about!

***

Uses

- Contemporary worship: *Guide included.*
- Youth or Seeker Bible study: *Guide included.*
- Adult study: *Guide included.*
  Use to train clergy or laity.
- Revival.
- Sermon during Pentecost.
- Traditional worship service.
- Use in a prison, homeless shelter, or crisis center.

The Revised Common Lectionary
    Year C, Sixth Sunday of Easter: Acts 16:9-15
    Year C, Seventh Sunday of Easter: Acts 16:16-34
    Year C, Sunday between June 12 and June 18 inclusive: Galatians 2:15-21

*Congregation invited to stand.
**The Faith We Sing
***The United Methodist Hymnal
****Draw Me Close: 25 Top Vineyard Worship Songs

1. "Love Came Down," performed by Lindell Cooley, in *Open Up the Sky, Hosanna! Music, 2001.* Also available in *Hosanna! Music Songbook 16.*
2. *Simon Birch*, written and directed by Mark Steven Johnson. (Hollywood Pictures Company, 1998). The movie is rated PG. The screenplay was adapted from the novel *A Prayer for Owen Meany* by John Irving.
3. "Dive," performed by Steven Curtis Chapman, on *Speechless*, Sparrow Records, 1999.

CHAPTER 7

Mary Fletcher: A Young Woman's Faith Leads to Holiness and Reform

By Brenda Motley Newman

Scripture: Acts 2:42-47

> **Stage Setting:** Place a rocking chair with an old wooden table beside it at the front of the worship area. Stack a Bible and older books on the table.
>
> **Props:** Rocking chair, Bible, books, old table.
>
> **Costume:** Early 1700s dress appropriate for a lady from a conservative, lower class family. Costume shops and college drama departments often rent time period costumes.
>
> **Presentation:** The presenter may sit in the rocker for the entire presentation or walk as she speaks, holding her diary.
>
> **Presentation time:** Eight to ten minutes.
>
> **Script placement:** Hide in black journal that serves as Mary's diary.

Script

(All lines in boldface type are excerpts from The Life of Mrs. Mary Fletcher by Henry Moore. Moore's biography is a compilation of Mary Fletcher's journals and other authentic documents.)[1]

"From my earliest years, I can remember the Spirit of God striving with me, and offering me salvation . . . when I was about four years old, I received such a conviction that God heareth prayer, that it often giveth much comfort to me even now in seasons of trial and danger . . . when I was five years old, I began to have much concern about my eternal welfare, and frequently inquired whether such and such things were sins."

It is an excerpt from my diary that I cherish. It was the beginning of my journey—a journey of faith—a journey pursuing holiness. Allow me to introduce myself. I am Mary Bosanquet (boh SAN kee) Fletcher. I was born in England in 1739. I chose a different course from most young women of my day. It was not the course my friends or my parents desired for me. My parents were wealthy and cultured. The pursuits of the day—theater, fashion, and fox-hunting—occupied most. My parents used to send me to visit with relatives, hoping these fashionable interests would sway me from my religious pursuits. But I was not thus persuaded. I saw that beside the growing wealth in society, there was also a growing apathy toward morals and values. The people at large were self-centered and so was the church. There was no concern for the poor or the needs of others. The Church of England was in need of reform. My search became a search for holiness.

My journey started with the influence of a servant maid who had joined the people called Methodists. I first thought I had to be a Methodist to be saved, but I learned that you are saved by believing. I listened in on every religious conversation before I was even old enough to be taught. I was drawn to prayer and study. When I was twenty-one, I realized the pain this search for holiness would bring. My father forbade me to convert my brothers, and I refused to cease sharing my faith. I was expelled from my home. I look back to my journal where I wrote with relief and fear:

"I am cast out of my father's house. I know the heart of a stranger . . . I cried unto the Lord, and found a sweet calm overspread my spirit."

I missed my family deeply, but I did visit and our relationship grew over the years. When they began to understand the call the Lord had given me, they helped support my work in later years. Now to tell you about the work the Lord called me to do. I began the first Methodist orphanage. A friend, Sarah Ryan, joined me, saying that the Lord had laid the burden on her as well. We had six children in the orphanage at first, but soon there were thirty-five children under our care. Daily we had worship, prayer, and lessons with them. Our home, however, became much more than just an orphanage. It became a meeting place for the societies John Wesley had started. It became a Methodist preaching house and a home for preachers when they were passing through. John Wesley even wrote of our house:

"O what a house of God is here! Not only for decency and order, but for the life and power of religion. I am afraid there are very few such to be found in all the king's dominion."

I spoke at many of the meetings and became a society leader and class leader. My interpretation of the Scriptures became rather widely known, and sometimes I received more attention than I desired.

You see, we Methodists were not well received. I still tremble when I remember the night four men with clubs interrupted a meeting in which I was speaking. By the grace of God, I kept right on speaking, and at the end, I gave them a copy of the Rules of the Society.

At one point, I had decided to remain single, but in 1781, I married John Fletcher. He was one of John Wesley's preachers, a Methodist preacher. We offered more services than we could really manage. My husband died not even a decade after we were married. My husband's illness and the illnesses among our parishioners made life unbearably hard. But my search for holiness never ceased. The Lord was closer to me than ever. After society meetings, many came to me giving a blessed account of how the Lord had given them the full assurance of peace and pardon! Even when my breath was labored and shallow, I could not help but speak. How the Lord blessed my life. A continuing burden on my heart concerned the people called Methodists. In one of my last journal entries, I had begun to see that we would never reform the Church of England.

"But I here declare, I have been joined to the people united to Mr. Wesley for above threescore years . . . The life of true religion is with them and the work increases . . .

I have always considered myself as a member of the Church of England, and so have the united friends. In some measure we are now pushed out. O let not one word of this be left out! What I mean by being pushed out is—the church minister has repeatedly expressed a wish that the Methodist should be a separate people; as he always thought it best for the Church of England and the people called Methodists to move in distinct lines."

[The preacher, or another speaker may conclude with: "Of course, Mary Fletcher did not know the long-term result of John Wesley's movement—a movement that did split off from the Church of England and is now a ten million plus-member denomination with congregations, missionaries, and mission work in abundance throughout the world. It started with a deep desire for a relationship with God, for holiness, and for inclusiveness. It was nurtured by the societies meeting together in prayer and study. It matured through acts of service such as Mary Fletcher's orphanage and ministries to serve the poor and those in need."]

(If this script is used during a service honoring older adults you may add: "We remember and thank all the saints who would not be swayed from religious pursuits and have striven to keep the church holy and keep us close to our Savior. We thank our older adults for their witness, their impact on the history of the church, and their mentoring of many individuals during their faith journeys. There are countless individuals like Mary Fletcher, male and female, young and old, who strengthened God's church throughout the generations. We thank God for each one of them this morning, and for each of you, for the lives you have touched and the hearts you warmed.")

Worship

Worship Bulletin
Fourth Sunday of Easter

(Suggestions for Heritage Sunday and Women's Sunday are included in this Order of Worship.)

Prelude

Bringing Light to the Church

Responsive Call to Worship:

> Leader: We come in search of holiness.
> **People: We only see glimpses of holiness at our jobs, at the ball fields, and in the nightly news.**
> Leader: Self-centeredness and greed are easy to find.
> **People: We long for generosity and mercy.**
> Leader: Apathy is commonplace.
> **People: We long for compassion and empathy.**
> Leader: Pride is everywhere.
> **People: We need to build each other up.**
> **All: We have come in search of holiness.**

* Hymn: #64 "Holy, Holy, Holy! Lord God Almighty" * * *

Words of Welcome

Church Family Concerns

Silent Prayer

Pastoral Prayer

Offering

  Special Music: #94 "Your Name is Holy"****

* Doxology: #94***

Reading from the Psalms: Psalm 23

Modern Day Psalm 23 Presentation: *(Invite youth to share modern day paraphrases of the Twenty-third Psalm. Prepare paraphrases in advance during a Sunday school hour or at a youth meeting.)*

Special Recognition: *(If this is Heritage Sunday, share church history. If this is Women's Sunday, invite women from your local group to share their ministries. Present plaques or pins at this time.)*

Praise Reports and Testimonies: *(If this is Heritage Sunday, ask for praise for a Sunday school teacher, youth leader, etc. from the past. If it is a Women's Sunday celebration, lift up praise for women leaders or ministries that women have undertaken.)*

Children's Choir: #558 "We Are the Church"***
  Or #451 "Be Thou My Vision"***

Children's Moment
  Suggestion 1: Bring pictures of activities the church has participated in during the past year. Ask the children to share something they have liked doing at church. **Ask:** What are some of the things you think the church can do that will make God smile?
  Suggestion 2: If it is Heritage Sunday, have an older member talk about Sunday school or worship when he or she was a child. If it is Women's Sunday, have a woman of the church share some of the ministries the women are involved in.

Scripture Lesson: Acts 2:42-47

Monologue

Hymn: #402 "Lord, I Want to Be a Christian"***

* Benediction: **"Lord, may we continue to search for holiness that our witness for you will pass on to future generations."**

Adult Bible Study

(Start with the discussion questions if used after the worship service. Or use as below.)

Open with Prayer

Scripture Reading: Acts 2:42-47

Monologue Presentation

Discussion Questions *(The following questions are lengthy. You are encouraged to reproduce them and hand them out to participants.)*

1. Mary Fletcher describes her journey as a journey pursuing holiness. Holiness is a theme in both traditional and contemporary Christian music. Popular traditional songs include "Holy, Holy, Holy" and "Silent Night, Holy Night," and popular contemporary selections include "Take My Life" and "Your Name is Holy," both in *Draw Me Close: 25 Top Vineyard Worship Songs. (If time permits, find these or other songs in advance and study their lyrics.)* **Ask:** How do you understand holiness? How would you explain holiness to a nonbeliever?

2. Mary Fletcher's concerns for the church included the lack of morals and the growing apathy in society. She was concerned that these trends seemed to have invaded the Church of England. She was saddened that the church had become self-centered and demonstrated little concern for the poor or for the needs of others. **Ask:** What concerns do you have for the church today? Provide an example of self-centeredness. Can you give examples of ways in which the church does exhibit concern for the poor and offer generosity?

3. Mary did not initially understand salvation, but learned a person is saved by believing. The book *John Wesley's Theology Today* by Colin W. Williams lifts up John Wesley's Order of Salvation: "Sometimes Wesley gives his outline of the order of salvation in a short summary, as in his famous: Our main doctrines, which include all the rest, are three—that of repentance, of faith, and of holiness. The first of these we account as it were, the porch of religion; the next, the door; the third, religion itself."[2]

Study the outline below:

A. **Repentance.** Look up Acts 2:38 and Acts 26:20. The word *repent* is often followed by the word *and* in scripture passages. Note the use of the word *and* in both of these passages in Acts. We are to repent *and* turn to God. Repentance is both expressing sorrow for sin *and* a desire to change. **Ask:** How do you understand repentance? How would you explain repentance to a nonbeliever?

B. **Faith.** Study Romans 3:21-26 and Romans 5:1. The word *justification* is used somewhat interchangeably with faith as the "door of religion." Paul says in Romans 5:1, "Therefore, since we are justified by faith." Justification is God's gift of forgiveness and our reliance on this forgiveness. This is where we open up our doors (our lives) and invite Christ to work in us. Wesley writes, "By justification we are saved from the guilt of sin, and restored to the favour of God."[3]

(Take a moment and silently reflect on your faith.) **Ask:** Are there doors in your life closed to God? Have you invited God into your heart? Where are you in your faith journey? *(Allow for silent prayer.)*

C. **Holiness.** Sanctification and Christian perfection are terms used somewhat interchangeably with holiness as the "house of religion." Wesley writes: "By sanctification we are saved from the power and root of sin, and restored to the image of God."[4] Sanctification is the process of becoming more and more within the will of God. It is the process of growing into Christ's likeness. **Ask:** What are some of the steps you and I need to take in order to grow into Christ's likeness? *(Study Acts 2:42 and note that the early disciples devoted themselves to teaching, fellowship, prayer, and the breaking of bread.)*

4. Mary Fletcher referred to the Rules of the Society. Wesley's original plan did not include the organization of a new church but rather an organization called the United Societies. It was meant to be a reform movement. The Society was the primary unit into which the Methodists gathered and Wesley emphasized accountability, watching over one another in love, study, and fellowship in these groups. These societies were formed in London, England, Ireland, Scotland, and the colonies in America. They continually nourished and fed the new believers and thus allowed the church to grow. Williams in *John Wesley's Theology Today* wrote:

> The only condition for entrance into these societies was a desire 'to flee from the wrath to come, to be saved from their sins,' but continuance in membership depended upon the acceptance of a life of discipline. This discipline was laid out in terms of the concrete situations of their daily lives, and the conditions were:
>
> (1) "doing no harm." As examples, Wesley spoke of the need to abstain from swearing, drunkenness, smuggling, extravagant dress, useless diversions, self-indulgence, miserliness.
> (2) "doing good," such as caring for men's bodies, especially the poor, the sick, and the distressed; caring for men's souls by instruction, exhortation, and reproof, with particular responsibility for those of the household of faith.
> (3) "attending upon all the ordinances of God." Those within the societies were expected to receive the ministrations of the great congregation by attending to the liturgy and sacraments of the Church.[5]

(The sacraments include baptism and Holy Communion.) These societies were used to encourage personal holiness in a group of committed disciples. **Ask:** How do our small groups, *(Sunday school, Bible studies, Stephen ministries, etc.)* compare today? There has been some resurgence of accountability groups modeled after Wesley's Societies. **Ask:** If your church formed such a group, would you be interested? Why or why not? What can we glean from these societies that is of current benefit?

Close with a prayer, seeking God's guidance for the church and for your own spiritual growth.

✳ ✳ ✳

Uses

- Traditional or blended worship: Use during the Easter season or for Heritage Sunday, "Senior Citizen's" Sunday or a Women's Sunday. It may also be used with an adult or youth confirmation class. *Order of Worship for Fourth Sunday of Easter included.*
- Women's Program or Retreat: Use as the program or as a discussion starter at a women's meeting.
- Methodism/Membership class: Use during a class on the history of Methodism or a Methodist membership class.
- Adult Bible study: *Guide included.*

The Revised Common Lectionary
Year A, Fourth Sunday of Easter: Acts 2:42-47.

*Congregation invited to stand.
**The Faith We Sing
***The United Methodist Hymnal
****Draw Me Close: 25 Top Vineyard Worship Songs

1. Henry Moore, *The Life of Mrs. Mary Fletcher* (London: J. Kershaw, 1824).
2. Colin W. Williams, *John Wesley's Theology Today* (Nashville: Abingdon Press, 1960), 39-40.
3. Ibid., 40
4. Ibid.
5. Ibid., 136-137.

CHAPTER 8

Storm-Tossed Family and Dried-Up Hope: Jesus' Power over Storms

By Brenda Motley Newman

Scripture: Luke 8:26-33

(Two brief monologues and prayers based on Luke 8:22-25, 26-33, and 42b-48)

Stage Setting: Place a simple chair at the front of the worship area. The presenter may stand or pace, without the addition of any props. The Bible may then be held in the speaker's hands. An alternate suggestion is to have the stage area decorated as a living room.

Props: Chair, Bible.

Costume: No costume needed. In "Dried-Up Hope," presenter wears casual clothing as if she is lounging around the house.

Presentation: Middle-aged females are the presenters. In "Dried-Up Hope," presenter props up with pillows on the couch if stage is set as a living room.

Script placement: In a Bible.

Scripts

A. Storm-Tossed Family
Scripture: Luke 8:22-25

The storms come up quickly. There is no early Doppler warning system at my house, no twenty-four hour weather channel. It doesn't matter whether the storm is thunder and lightning or hurricane-force winds. It still seems to come out of nowhere, tearing through the fabric of our relationships and leaving devastation in its wake.

I had just come home from church last night. It had been a great evening. We had a fired-up speaker from one of the fastest-growing churches in the nation. And he was firing us up. I had lingered after the service sharing my excitement and new ideas with others. But goodness knows, my own family could benefit from some firing up or even a good old-fashioned revival. I can barely even get them to make their way to church on Sunday mornings.

I knew something was not quite right when I walked in. Andrew's music wasn't blaring from the basement. Jeff, my husband, and our youngest son, Matt, were not at their usual arguing. The TV wasn't even turned on. I found the three of them seated on the couch in the living room. Matt's eyes were red. Jeff motioned for me to sit down. His words are still a blur . . . something about my parents in an accident and that we needed to go to the hospital immediately.

It was four hours later when I found myself sitting in the chapel at the hospital. There were so many tubes, and the doctor's words were also a blur: "serious condition . . . we are doing all we can . . . we will know more in the next twenty-four hours." I tried unsuccessfully to pray. I don't know how long I sat there before Andrew and Matt joined me. Matt snuggled up to me like he used to do before teenage hormones took residence in his growing frame. None of us said anything. Jeff slipped beside me and rested his arm on my shoulder. I picked up a Bible. I opened it, thinking I would find a psalm to read. But it opened to Luke 8:22.

> One day he got into a boat with his disciples, and he said to them, "Let us go across to the other side of the lake." So they put out, and while they were sailing he fell asleep. A windstorm swept down on the lake, and the boat was filling with water, and they were in danger. They went to him and woke him up, shouting, "Master, Master, we are perishing!" And he woke up and rebuked the wind and the raging waves; they ceased, and there was a calm. He said to them, "Where is your faith?" They were afraid and amazed, and said to one another, "Who then is this, that he commands even the winds and the water, and they obey him?"

Jeff had his head down. Matt was crying. Andrew remained as stiff as the pews we were sitting on. I prayed, **"Master, Master, the boat is full of water. We have been a storm-tossed family for too long. This latest storm is too fierce. Help us. Wake up, Lord."** *(The presenter invites the congregation to join in the unison prayer found in the bulletin.)*

Unison Prayer:

    Lord, we pray today for those caught in the midst of storms. We pray for those caught in unexpected storms, the storms that shake our foundations and leave us breathless and desperate. We pray for those who live in the midst of daily storms, the storms that threaten our security and well-being. Lord, some of our relationships are stormy, and some areas in our lives need guidance. Restore our relationships and grant us wisdom and direction. We are consumed at times, Lord, by storms of self-will or self-hatred. We are perishing, Master. Our boats are full of water. We are in danger. Wake up, Lord.

    Lord, we pray today for those caught in the midst of natural disasters— earthquakes, hurricanes, tornadoes, floods, and fires. Give these families material and spiritual resources to rebuild their homes and their lives. Hear their desperate cries for help. Thank you for the advances made in predicting weather patterns and your help in organizing relief teams. Continue to motivate us that we will reach out to others in their times of need. Through Jesus Christ our Lord, who rebukes the wind and raging waves, and they cease. Amen.

B. Dried-Up Hope
Scripture: Luke 8:42b-48

My husband asked me last night if I needed him to turn out the light. I mumbled something, but the truth of the matter is that I had not even noticed the light. I lie in bed so much during the day that night and day have blended. Weeks run into months, and when I tried to write a check the other day, I was startled that I was not certain what year it was.

I stopped to count and realized that it has been twelve years. Twelve years since the pain in my body became so severe that I gave up work. I tried going to a part-time position, but I couldn't even keep up with a few responsibilities. Our financial resources dried up quickly once we were reduced to one income and overwhelmed by endless doctor bills. We went to every specialist on the East *and* the West Coast. Then our hope dried up as well. After twelve years, there is no diagnosis, no name attached to my chronic, handicapping pain.

I have tried herbal cures, chiropractors, and psychiatrists. I even hired a spiritual guru for a month or two, but the guru ran out on me before our money ran out. I cannot remember the last time I had lunch with a friend. I cannot remember the last wedding I attended. I have not been to a baby shower, a birthday party, or even shopping for at least a year.

I picked up the family Bible off the table in the living room this morning. It was part of my inheritance when Grandmother passed away. Unfortunately, I did not inherit her strong faith. The weight of the book increased the aching sensation in my arms, yet I opened it to the Gospel According to Luke. Why Luke? I have no idea. It was chapter eight. I started reading at the end of verse 42.

> As he went, the crowds pressed in on him. Now there was a woman who had been suffering from hemorrhages for twelve years; and though she had spent all she had on physicians, no one could cure her. She came up behind him and touched the fringe of his clothes, and immediately her hemorrhage stopped. Then Jesus asked, "Who touched me?" When all denied it, Peter said, "Master, the crowds surround you and press in on you." But Jesus said, "Someone touched me; for I noticed that power had gone out from me." When the woman saw that she could not remain hidden, she came trembling; and falling down before him, she declared in the presence of all the people why she had touched him, and how she had been immediately healed. He said to her, "Daughter, your faith has made you well; go in peace."

(The presenter closes the Bible and pauses a moment.)

Buried deep within the recesses of my soul, I felt the stirring of hope. If only I could touch the hem of Jesus' robe. *(The presenter invites the congregation to join together in the unison prayer found in the bulletin.)*

Unison Prayer:

Lord, be with all today who suffer with illness. Be especially with those who suffer from chronic conditions that have plagued them for years. Be with the families who care for them. Bless the research of those who search for cures. Help us to trust in the great mystery of your love. Help us to trust that your desire for each of us is health and wholeness. Grant us the faith to reach out to touch the hem of your robe. Grant us the faith to take your hand when you reach out to us. Through Jesus Christ, the Master Physician, we pray. Amen.

Worship

Worship Bulletin
A Service of Healing

Prelude

Bringing Light to the Church

(Invite people from all generations to read.)

Reader One: "Are any among you sick? They should call for the elders of the church and have them pray over them, anointing them with oil in the name of the Lord." (James 5:14)

Reader Two: "Bear one another's burdens, and in this way you will fulfill the law of Christ." (Galatians 6:2)

Reader Three: "When he went ashore, he saw a great crowd; and he had compassion for them and cured their sick." (Matthew 14:14)

Reader Four: "He heals the brokenhearted, and binds up their wounds." (Psalm 147:3)

* Opening Hymn: #2177 "Wounded World that Cries for Healing"**

Welcome: We welcome you to today's service of healing. Jesus spent much of his ministry healing the estranged and sick. He called his disciples to ministries of healing and calls each of us to trust him for healing and to pray for and anoint the sick. God heals in a variety of ways, including the gifts God gives to those in the various fields of medicine. A healing service is not magic and not a promise of cure. It is calling on God's promises to be with us during suffering, to provide us with courage and comfort, and to save us from sin and death. We come with a variety of needs. These needs are physical, emotional, mental, relational, or spiritual. As Christians, we recognize that the greatest healing is a reconciled relationship with God and one another.

Reading from the Psalms: Psalm 130

* Hymn: #262 "Heal Me, Hands of Jesus"***

Offering

* Doxology: #94***

Children's Moment
(Show pictures of different kinds of hardships. Examples would include stormy weather, people in the hospital or nursing home, an individual crying, a car wreck.)
Share: Sometimes sad things happen. We are reading from the Bible this morning about people who experienced hard times, like a bad storm or sickness. *(Read the story of the storm at sea or a healing story from a children's Bible.)* **Share:** Jesus wants to help us when we are sick or during any kind of hard time. *(Give each of the children a "survival kit" for hard times. These can be self-sealing plastic bags with adhesive bandages, a prayer on an index card, and a small flashlight enclosed.)* Close with a prayer.

STORM-TOSSED FAMILY AND DRIED-UP HOPE: JESUS' POWER OVER STORMS

Meditations on Luke 8:22-25, 26-33, 42b-48

(These verses proclaim Jesus' power over nature, demons, and illness
The passages are not read in advance of the monologues.)

Monologue 1: "Storm-Tossed Family"

Unison Prayer: (Print words in the bulletin to prayer found in monologue.)

Reader: *(Luke 8:26-33)*

> Then they arrived at the country of the Gerasenes, which is opposite Galilee. As he stepped out on land, a man of the city who had demons met him. For a long time he had worn no clothes, and he did not live in a house but in the tombs. When he saw Jesus, he fell down before him and shouted at the top of his voice, "What have you to do with me, Jesus, Son of the Most High God? I beg you, do not torment me"— for Jesus had commanded the unclean spirit to come out of the man. (For many times it had seized him; he was kept under guard and bound with chains and shackles, but he would break the bonds and be driven by the demon into the wilds.) Jesus then asked him, "What is your name?" He said, "Legion"; for many demons had entered him. They begged him not to order them to go back into the abyss. Now there on the hillside a large herd of swine was feeding; and the demons begged Jesus to let them enter these. So he gave them permission. Then the demons came out of the man and entered the swine, and the herd rushed down the steep bank into the lake and was drowned.

Prayer for Healing:

  Leader: Lord, be with us in all of our struggles. Be with all who struggle with depression. Restore to all the gift of joy.

SILENT PRAYERS

  Leader: Lord, be with all who struggle with fear. Increase our faith, Lord, and decrease our fear.

SILENT PRAYERS

  Leader: Lord, be with all who struggle with unrelenting anxiety. Grant us inward peace.

SILENT PRAYERS

  Leader: Lord, be with all who struggle with compulsive behavior and mental illness. Heal us, Lord.

SILENT PRAYERS

  Leader: Lord, be with the caregivers of those who suffer from mental illness.

SILENT PRAYERS

> **Leader:** Lord, lead those in the fields of psychology and psychiatry to new understandings and more effective treatments.

SILENT PRAYERS

> **Leader:** Lord, be with us as we struggle with our legion of demons. Through Jesus Christ our Lord who commands unclean spirits to leave. Amen.

Monologue 2: "Dried-Up Hope"

Unison Prayer for Healing: *(Print words in bulletin to prayer found in monologue.) A Service of Healing. (Use "A Service of Healing" from* The United Methodist Book of Worship, *pp. 615-621. The choir may sing or lead the congregation in singing #2213 "Healer of Our Every Ill"** and #2215"Cares Chorus"**during the time of anointing.)*

* Hymn: #375 "There Is a Balm in Gilead"***

* Benediction: **"May God hold you tenderly and grant you healing and peace."**

❋ ❋ ❋

Adult Bible Study

Scripture: James 5:14-16 and Luke 8:22-25, 26-33, 42b-48

(Use the study after a worship service in which the monologues were presented, or present as below. If used after a worship service, ask questions 1 to 4 consecutively, then continue with the study of James 5:14-16.)

Open with prayer.

Present Monologue 1 with Unison Prayer
1. Most of us have been overwhelmed by forces beyond our control, thus we find this story of the storm at sea particularly engaging. **Say:** Name forces in nature and society that seem beyond our control. What message of assurance does this passage offer when we are in such circumstances? *(That God is with us, that God cares, that God has power over storms.)*
2. In biblical times, the sea represented chaos. God created order out of chaos. **Ask:** What chaos in your life needs God's ordering?

Assign someone to read Luke 8:26-33. Share in the prayer for healing found in the worship outline.
3. In Jesus' day, people understood the world to be populated by demons and spirits. **Ask:** How do you understand demons today? What would you include on a list of demons? How does mental illness fit into your picture of demons?

Present Monologue 2 with Unison Prayer.
4. We observe Jesus moving toward the demoniac and the hemorrhaging woman. He did not avoid or move away from them, but rather ignored the rituals of the day that would have considered both unclean. He was filled with compassion and acted on his compassion. **Ask:** Do you observe the church moving toward

the ill with compassion or avoiding them? What are opportunities for greater compassion in our community and in the church?

Assign someone to read James 5:14-16. **Share:** This passage from James is often used at the beginning of a Service of Healing.

5. Verses 14-16 of James's speech deals with the sick and the community's response to those who are ill. In biblical times, the sick were often alienated because of fear that contact would spread the illness. **Ask:** What are some of society's fears that alienate the sick today?

Those who suffer chronic conditions sometimes become forgotten over time. Think of those in your church community who are no longer active because of illness. **Ask:** What are specific ways the church is ministering to these individuals?

If you have taken care of a loved one with a chronic or recurring condition, can you remember a time when you felt resentment because the illness prevented you from participating in other activities or kept you from completing personal goals? **Ask:** How can the church community support and assist caregivers? Brainstorm ideas and list them on a board or large sheet of paper. Present them at a future board meeting or appropriate nurture committee of the church.

6. In verse 14, James empowers the sick by writing that they themselves are to summon the elders. As a society, we teach people to speak up for their needs. **Say:** Give examples of times when we need to encourage this empowerment of the sick. On a personal note, in what ways do you strive to be assertive in your own medical care? James specifically notes that the purpose for which the sick are to summon the elders is to pray for them and to anoint them with oil. **Ask:** Does the church encourage the sick to specifically request prayer and anointing? Have healing services been a part of your church experience?

7. In verse 16, James refers to the sickness of the community, not just individual sickness. James implies that confession and intercessory prayer are necessary for healing. This implication maintains a connection between physical and spiritual illness. It also makes the connection between healing and right relationships.

Close with time spent in silent prayer, reflecting on relationships in your personal life and in the life of the church that need to be restored.

✳ ✳ ✳

Uses

- Traditional or contemporary worship: Use two monologues together. Use at any season of the church year.
- Service of Healing: *Order of Worship included.* (Purchase olive oil.) Especially recommended for a midweek service.
- Adult Bible study: *Guide included.*
- Retreat or other group setting with the focus of healing.
- Support group for caregivers.

The Revised Common Lectionary
    Year C, Sunday between June 19 and 25 inclusive: Luke 8:26-39

*Congregation invited to stand.
**The Faith We Sing
***The United Methodist Hymnal
****Draw Me Close: 25 Top Vineyard Worship Songs

CHAPTER 9

Margaret: A Grieving Mother Yearns for Her Wayward Son

By Brenda Motley Newman

Scripture: Hosea 11:1-11

Stage Setting; Place a rocking chair with table beside it at the front of the worship area. Put a Bible and childhood items on the table.

Props: Rocking chair, table, childhood items such as balls, trophies, photo album.

Costume: Everyday clothing.

Presentation: The presenter starts by picking up the photo album, then sits in the rocker, opens the album, and begins.

Presentation time: Fifteen minutes.

Script placement: In the photo album.

Script

Margaret: I remember his first steps. The cat had climbed on the windowsill, and he kept saying "tat, tat" with each shaky step. Memories—sweet and bittersweet—are etched in my mind forever. I could rock him for hours and then lift him up to my cheeks, where his soft skin matched his soft breathing sighs. *(Rock gently.)* Then I could lay him in his crib without ever waking him. His easygoing, compliant nature deceived me into believing that rebellion was the least of my worries.

The first time we took him swimming, he was so excited I could barely hold him. His arms and legs flailed and kicked every which way. Little squeals of delight rang out every time he touched the water. He stood by the back door daily, hand on the doorknob, waiting to be taken outside. *(Hold hand up and twist as if turning a doorknob and then hold up three fingers to indicate three tricycles.)* He went through three tricycles before we ever made it to the bicycle with training wheels. He could ride for hours.

Deep blue was the color of the shirt he wore the first day of kindergarten. I remember the color because it matched the deep blue in my heart. I grieved with every step he took toward the sturdy brick building. School parties, field days, and end-of-year assemblies marked his growth, just as we marked the inches on the wall as he became taller. *(Pretend to mark lines as if on a growth chart.)* Each year, the lessons were harder, both in the classroom and in life. I held him as he sobbed uncontrollably after he was excluded from the playground activities by the "in" crowd of boys. *(Cross arms as if hugging, but then cross tightly as if offended.)* Yet, he was brave and tried again and made his own friends.

We cheered him on at every Little League game and pouted with him as he sat on the bench throughout his brief football stints during middle school and high school. The lump in my throat from the first time he drove the car by himself is still stuck there.

(Place hand on throat momentarily.) And I swell with pride, even now, as I remember him all dressed up in his tuxedo waiting for the limousine he rented for the prom.

I just recently put away the first aid kit that sat obediently over the sink for two decades. His dad and I joked that he had more cuts and scrapes than there were grains of sand on the beach. And I would have a bigger bank account if I could collect all the money I paid to doctors for sore throats, earaches, stomach viruses, and bike wrecks.

Of course, I would have spent every cent I ever made to take care of him. That's just how a parent loves a child. Now I wish that money, or a doctor's visit, or a bedtime story could put things right again. *(Shake head back and forth gently.)* We taught him right from wrong. He spent enough time grounded in his room . . . he had enough privileges taken away . . . he missed enough outings with his buddies to have learned that there are consequences for poor choices.

I don't know when the rebellion started. *(Shrug shoulders helplessly.)* I didn't see any pattern of disobedience. Yes, he made some poor choices along the way, but we corrected him immediately. And then he would do better for a while. I heard a preacher once comparing us to sheep, the image Jesus uses. He painted this picture in my mind. He said that most sheep just nibble themselves lost. They don't take off all at once. They just find some grass that tastes especially sweet, and they keep on eating and don't pay attention to where they are. Before they know it, they've wandered away from the flock, and they don't know how to find their way home.

I don't believe our son intended for his life to be the way it is. But I don't think he is ready to change either. The consequences of the path he has chosen may be eternal. How can I let him go? How can I bear the thought of being separated from him forever? He does know his way home, but will he ever return? *(Pick up the Bible.)*

The yearning in my heart, I think, is a small glimpse of the yearning God has in his heart for my son and for all of God's children who are lost. I think I began to understand when I read a passage from Hosea. Listen to God's yearning as I read Hosea 11:1-11.

> When Israel was a child, I loved him, and out of Egypt I called my son. The more I called them, the more they went from me; they kept sacrificing to the Baals, and offering incense to idols. Yet it was I who taught Ephraim to walk, I took them up in my arms; but they did not know that I healed them. I led them with cords of human kindness, with bands of love. I was to them like those who lift infants to

their cheeks. I bent down to them and fed them. They shall return to the land of Egypt, and Assyria shall be their king, because they have refused to return to me. The sword rages in their cities, it consumes their oracle-priests, and devours because of their schemes. My people are bent on turning away from me. To the Most High they call, but he does not raise them up at all. How can I give you up, Ephraim? How can I hand you over, O Israel? How can I make you like Admah? How can I treat you like Zeboiim? My heart recoils within me; my compassion grows warm and tender. I will not execute my fierce anger; I will not again destroy Ephraim; for I am God and no mortal, the Holy One in your midst, and I will not come in wrath. They shall go after the LORD, who roars like a lion; when he roars, his children shall come trembling from the west. They shall come trembling like birds from Egypt, and like doves from the land of Assyria; and I will return them to their homes, says the LORD.

Can you hear all the ways God loves us? *It was I who taught you to walk, took you in my arms, healed you . . . Yet you are bent on turning away from me . . . How can I give you up?*

Do you hear the way a parent's love is modeled after God's love for us? I guess this is partly what it means to be created in God's image. God's love is the **creative love** that brought us into existence. Who can forget the day your child was born? He or she is a part of you. Then the days are filled with teaching—**instructive love**. God, through God's Word, teaches us how to live. In Hosea, we hear the grief as God cries out, *It was I who taught you to walk*. It is a **tolerant love**, allowing a child to make mistakes and then holding your arms out in forgiveness. It is a **healing love**, bandaging knees and hearts. The Lord exclaims in Hosea, *"I took them up in my arms, but they did not know that I healed them."* It is a **corrective love**, intervening when a child has wandered too far off the path.[1]

This is what God does for us. God's grief must surely match mine. Every night, the news is full of abandoned babies, abused children, domestic violence, the latest murders, and the latest argument between boards and officials.

I don't know if I can carry my grief any longer. How in the world does God carry all the grief from each of us?

It is the last image of God given in this passage that stays with me now. It is verse 10, *"They shall go after the Lord, who roars like a lion; when he roars, his children shall come trembling from the west. They shall come trembling . . . and I will return them to their homes."* It is not the comforting image of the Lord as our Shepherd. It is not Jesus as the Bread of Life. But it is the image of God as a roaring lion. We are rebellious children, loved but delinquent. Time and again, everybody strays. I know I have. I have gone to church to hear God's Word, but distractions kept me from listening. As a church, we fellowship with one another, but some still feel excluded and left out.

At church, we talk about the physical and spiritual needs of the community, but we leave with no plans designed to meet them. We hear God's call to generous giving and disciplined lives, but keep on living selfishly. God's roar is justified. God does not overlook our sin. God punishes us because God will not tolerate the ways we hurt ourselves and each other. But God does not punish us in anger, because vengeful anger only destroys. God disciplines us in love. God's wrath is a wrath of love—not a wrath that destroys good, as hate, envy, or unbridled anger can.

God yearns for us, a wayward children. God cries out, *"The more I called them, the more they went from me."* Hasn't every parent been there? You help your child decide the best way to handle their latest dilemma, and then they do the exact opposite. The more you reach out to them, the more they pull away. I can't recall the exact moment when my husband and I became roaring lions, but we did. Our tolerant and patient love became overshadowed by corrective love. We knew our son was straying so far off the path that drastic measures were needed. We issued our roar, but he has not come trembling back yet.

God's roar does not echo through the valleys of our lives and come back empty. This is the hope I cling to. Hosea reminds us, *The people will come back to God and God will return them to their homes.* This is the picture of hope and healing painted for us throughout God's Word. This is the prodigal son returning home to his father's open arms. This is the disciple Peter, who betrayed his Lord, being accepted again and then given the greatest of responsibilities. It is sins forgiven and new beginnings.

My prayer is that our son will hear God's roar and come home trembling to the love God wants to pour over him. My hope is that he will come home to our open arms. My prayer is that all who are lost will find the healing of God's open arms and second chances. *(Close with the prayer found in the bulletin outline.)*

Worship

Worship Bulletin

Prelude

Bringing Light to the Church

* Opening Hymn: #139 "Praise to the Lord, the Almighty" * * *

Words of Welcome

Praise Reports and Testimonies

* Gospel Reading: John 3:16 (Read by a child.)

Adult and Children's Choir: #2233 "Where Children Belong" * *

Hymn of Praise: #140 "Great Is Thy Faithfulness" * * *

Church Family Concerns

Silent Prayer

Pastoral Prayer

The Lord's Prayer

Offering:

    Special Music: #2 "Arms of Love" * * * *

* Doxology: #94 * * *

Children's Moment
- **Suggestion 1:** *(Bring a picture of a fence or a piece of broken wood to introduce the story.)*

"The Broken Fence"
By Brenda Motley Newman

It was my aunt's first instruction: "Now, Julia, don't climb on the fence, or even lean on it. The fence is old."

There were other instructions as well. Don't go inside the fences where the cows are. Don't bother Uncle Ned when he is on the tractor. It was my first visit to Aunt Ruby's farm. My sister and I were to stay for a whole week. I had been excited about it, but now I just wanted to go home. Would Aunt Ruby find out what I had done? I shut the door to the bedroom and threw myself across the bed and sobbed. Why hadn't I listened? The fence didn't look that old. How was I to know it would break if I stood on it for a second? I had just wanted to see over the hill to where Uncle Ned was plowing.

My older sister Millie came in and made things worse by trying to comfort me. "What's wrong Julia? Are you homesick? Do you want to call Mom?" How could I tell her I had broken the fence? I asked her to leave and told her I would be okay.

At supper, it was the first thing Aunt Ruby said after we were served. "Ned, I noticed a broken place in the fence on the west side of the house. You'll need to fix it tomorrow." I tried to eat after that, but I couldn't. I excused myself. I overheard Millie telling Aunt Ruby, "I think she's homesick. She'll be better tomorrow."

I woke up to the sound of Uncle Ned hammering. I looked out our bedroom window and saw Uncle Ned repairing the fence. I knew I had to tell the truth. I slipped on my jeans, and ran downstairs. Aunt Ruby was just coming into the kitchen. "Aunt Ruby, I have to tell you something." Before she could even respond, I blurted out, "I broke the fence. I didn't mean to. I should have listened to you. I just wanted to see over the hill. I'm sorry Aunt Ruby."

Aunt Ruby smiled at me and gave me a quick hug. "It's okay, Julia. I'm glad you weren't hurt. Thank you for telling what happened. Why don't you go help Uncle Ned repair it?"

I ran out of the kitchen, feeling a hundred pounds lighter. Uncle Ned handed me a hammer, and I went to work.

Ask: How did Julia feel after she broke the fence? Why didn't she tell Aunt Ruby about it right away? How did Julia feel after she told Aunt Ruby? Did Aunt Ruby love Julia any less because she made a mistake? **Share:** We all make poor decisions sometimes. Our parents, grandparents, and friends understand and continue to love us. God also loves us even though we disobey and disappoint him at times. We are studying a scripture today from Hosea. It tells us that God waits for us to come after we have made mistakes because God loves us so much.

Close with a prayer:
"Dear God, thank you for loving us so much. Thank you for loving us when we make mistakes or when we do something wrong. Help us to forgive others when they make mistakes. Amen."

Children's Moment:
- **Suggestion 2**: Read *Love You Forever* by Robert Munsch.[2] This can be found in most bookstores.

Scripture Lesson: Hosea 11:1-11

Monologue

Prayer: (Unison)

"Dear God, Thank you for your creative love which brought us into existence. Thank you for your instructive love, your Word, and your Spirit which guide us daily. Thank you for your patient love when we get caught up with every new attraction the world offers. Thank you for your forgiving love when we come to you with all of our brokenness. Thank you for your healing love, which patches up both our knees and our hearts. Thank you for searching for us when we are lost, and bringing us back home. Amen."

* Closing Hymn: #357 "Just as I Am, Without One Plea" * * *

* Bringing Light to the World

* Benediction

* * *

Adult Bible Study

(Start with the discussion questions if used after the worship service. Or use as below.)

Open the lesson with prayer.

Monologue presentation.

Discussion Questions: *(Encourage participants to keep Bibles open to Hosea 11.)*
1. In Hosea 11, God is portrayed as a caring parent. **Ask:** What are the qualities of God lifted up in this image of the caring parent? Describe how these images of God affect you.
2. In Hosea 11, the Israelites are portrayed as a rebellious son, a son who disowns his parents. **Ask:** Who is then responsible for the rebellious behavior? Name times you have been tempted to take responsibility for your children's actions, instead of insisting that they accept their own responsibility. In your faith journey, think of times when you have accepted responsibility for your own rebellious behavior. Think of times when you have tried to shift the blame. **Ask:** What is the faith consequence for not accepting responsibility? How do you see this affecting your relationship with God?
3. In this text, God struggles with anger, grief, and disappointment with a wayward child, yet will not give up on him. **Ask:** How have you balanced your disappointment and sustaining active love for your children in the past?
4. Review each of the types of love described in the monologue. The monologue shared types of love that we offer our children. Study the following types and definitions of love.

Instructive love: a love that teaches a child to become a better person and to strive for the common good.

Patient love: a love that allows a child to make mistakes and accepts that child back in forgiveness.

Unconditional love: a love that is sustained in spite of the child's waywardness.

Corrective love: a love that intervenes when a child is straying too far.

Healing love: a love that assists in bringing a rebellious child to wholeness.

(Name appropriate times to offer each of these types of love to your child/children. Share some incidents when you have effectively displayed these types of love.)

5. In Hosea 11, it is God's roar that finally brings the rebellious one back home. There is healing because the lost are found. **Ask:** Can you remember a time in your life when you heard God's roar and came trembling back home? How can this comfort you in regard to your own child/children?

• **Close** the lesson with the prayer found in the worship outline or with personal prayers for those in attendance. Invite participants to lift up children, grandchildren, nieces, nephews, children of friends, or others for whom you feel concern.

✳ ✳ ✳

Uses

• Traditional or contemporary worship: Use at any season during the church year. Use with the theme of God's Forgiveness. *Order of Worship included.*

• Sunday school class on parenting or support groups for parents: Use as a lesson on the different types of parental love.

• Adult Bible study: *Guide included.*

The Revised Common Lectionary
    Year C, Sunday between July 31 and August 6 inclusive: Hosea 11:1-11

*Congregation invited to stand.
**The Faith We Sing
***The United Methodist Hymnal
****Draw Me Close: 25 Top Vineyard Worship Songs

---

1. These types of love are discussed in *The New Interpreter's Bible* (Nashville: Abingdon Press, 1996), 2:279.
2. Robert Munsch, *Love You Forever* (Canada: Firefly Books Ltd., 1999).

CHAPTER 10

Mattie May: A Mountain Woman's Tale of a Gracious Plenty

By Karen Farish Miller

Scripture: John 6:1-13

Stage setting: On a small altar or table are some sardines and biscuits and a small leather bag. Have a large bowl of green beans and a big pot. The covering on the altar is a rough cloth.

Costume: 1950s style belted shirtdress, horn-rim glasses, a sweater, socks and loafers. Her hair is brushed back off her face.

Presentation time:

Short version: Four minutes

Long version: Seven minutes

Script Placement: Put the script in the bowl of green beans. The presenter snaps the beans and puts them in the big pot while presenting the monologue.

Production notes: Mattie May is from the southern Appalachian mountains. Her words and phrases reflect her unique heritage. Although contemporary society has become sensitive to many minority groups, there are still many stereotypes related to mountain people. In television, cartoons, and movies, mountain people are rarely featured as honest, wise, witty, hardworking, and faith-filled people. Mattie May embodies all of these qualities.

A presenter who does not naturally speak with a southern dialect, and even some who do, may be tempted to exaggerate the southern vocal patterns to make the audience laugh at the character. This will cause Mattie May to become a caricature instead of a character. Before performing this monologue, practice it aloud many times.

Many southerners occasionally end sentences with the vocal inflection that goes up like a question, instead of down like a statement. In the script, question marks are occasionally inserted at the end of sentences that may not seem to be questions to assist the speaker with the proper inflection.

Where the monologue uses words, idioms, or pronunciations that may be unique to Appalachia or the South, words in parenthesis have been provided to explain a meaning or provide an alternative word choice.[1]

Script

My name is Mattie May and I live over in the next holler (neighborhood). What I'm aiming (trying) to tell ya may take a while so just get comfy (comfortable) and set a spell (sit for a while.)

Monday evening I took my checks over to the post office to mail. Ya know how they's posters and such tacked up on them winders next to the post office? Well, next to the posters of missin' children and such was a small 'nouncement. Maybe you caught a gander (look) at it? It was nuthin' fancy, hit just said, "Jesus, April 11, Lumpy Mountain."

I said to myself, "That's today!" It's not such a fur piece (long way) to Lumpy Mountain, so I carried my kids up the mountain to see whut wuz going on. All the way up the mountain I'm gettin' hungry. I start day dreamin' bout goin' to the Rock Café in town and settin' down before a plate a pork chops, cornbread, and collard greens. Purt (pretty) soon I could imagine the smell of it all cookin' up, jest as nice as you please. I say to myself, "If that preacher ain't any good, I'm goin' to the Rock Café."

When I get up there, I find out it's an honest-to-goodness outdoor revival. People are settin' in the grass listenin' to this preacher jawing (talking) bout how if you put God's kingdom first, you've have everythin' you shore nuff (really) need.

This preacher stops for a spell and says, "Peter!" Up walks this big handsome guy with muscles out to here. *(Gesture with hand to indicate a large muscle.)* He says, "Peter, where we gonna get the bread to feed all a these here people?" He had a gleam in his eye when he said it, and I wadn't sure if he was askin' a honest-to-goodness question or trickin' the man.

Anywho (Anyway), it's clear they've not got any food. You know what I'm thinkin', don't ya? "Good heavens to Betsy, Rock Café must be closed. There goes my pork chops!"

This guy called Peter says, "Jesus, I couldn't make enough money in six months to feed this crowd."

I reckon (guess) those that climbed that mountain before me and set outside a couple a hours were plum starving if they ain't took (haven't taken) a drink or had a bit a nothing. So up comes this boy what's been fishin' in a stream nearby? He's got a poke (sack) with some biscuits his mama give him and some small dried fish. That's hit. One of the men takes him to the preacher.

He says to Jesus, "This here boy has some biscuits and fish, but he's the only one that brung somethin'." (Only one who has brought anything.) So the preacher takes them five biscuits and them two puny fish and prays over 'em. And he gives 'em out to the crowd and the people start passin' 'em hand over hand until everbody has some. *(Pause.)* You catch whut I said? I said, everbody has some! My chillen' are poking me in the side goin', "Ask him how he done that. How'd he feed all them people with them piddlin little biscuits and fish? Does that preacher know magic or something?"

When they're done passin' the biscuits and fish to the people, there were parts of biscuits left over! I couldn't believe my eyes. I 'spect (suspect) some of them musta had some food hid and pulled it out. How else could this've happened?

Just then a light bub goes off in my head. That preacher had been a-talkin' bout how if you believe in God, you're bound to have everything that you shore nuff need? Even though there wasn't nuff food at the start, that little fella give all he had and God made it a gracious plenty. Hit got me a-thinkin' about how many times I say to myself, "Mattie May, you can't do that! You ain't got the smarts, or the money, or the time."

Ever now and then I gets talked into doin' something' and I end up settin' there thinkin', "I ain't got what it takes." Sometimes with them chillin (children) I think to myself, "Their mama's been beat up by life, and they should have better. I hope I ain't runt (haven't ruined) their lives."

But I'm like that kid with them fish? All I got is whut's in my poke. I'm a-feared it ain't enough. But in the hands of that Jesus preacher, two fish and five biscuits become enough. You trust God and what wasn't enough, is enough!

I don't know if this hits you up the side of the head like it done me, but I learnt somethin' up on that mountain. I learnt to get shed (rid) of those ideas about what's enough. I reckon God's enough, and I'll just give him my little bit to work with.

(This is the ending of the short version of this monologue.)

Hit's kinda like my quiltin' group when we started gettin' together in the back of Mr. Harman's store? Wadn't one of us had enough scraps to make a quilt worth sewin'. But when Idar (Ida) and her sister brung theirs and Esther brung what she had and I dug up what was left from the kids' Sunday clothes, we had us enough for a nice quilt.

Now you ast any one of us if we thought we coulda come up with it, we'd have laughed you out of the county. But we done it, each giving what we had. Now you take Idar there? She's faithful as the day is long and she's steady as a mule. But you couldn't pay her to get up in front of a bunch of people to say two words. No sir. She'd just as soon jump into the crick on a snowy day in February as stand up and talk. But she can make the best sweet 'tater pie this side of the Mississippi River.

Her sister ain't got a lick a book learnin' (formal education), but she's one of the smartest people I ever knowed. She has more stories that tell about why life is like it is than anybody. Her husband died a while back, but he was one of the most kindly hearted men you've ever want at meet. Oh, not so's you'd know it. On the outside, he was this big gruff fella who looked like he could pull down trees with his bare hands. But he was always a-haulin' wood for the wider (widow) woman next door, or takin' the feller in the next holler to the doctor, or gettin' the snow off old Mr. McFarlin's front steps so he wouldn't fall down when he come out to get the mail.

These are the people who make a big difference in our neck of the woods cuz they give whut they have and don't hold back nothin'. They let God do the rest. Here's the question I been astin' myself. If I was that boy up on the mountain, would I be willin' to give up my lunch for them people? If ya stop and think, all of us done been there, ain't we? Somebody dies and we walk up to the door with our little cassyrole (casserole) and a bottle a Cocacoly (Coca-Cola) wonderin' what in creation we can possibly say to make the family stop hurtin' so bad. And the door opens and we put our arms around 'em and suddenly without sayin' a word, we've done enough.

Or you join the choir knowin' you've got a voice that would run the cows off the farm, and you're too 'shamed to open your mouth? Then the music begins and you find you can keep up and you enjoy it and the people enjoy it. And we've done enough.

I 'member one time when my child was sick and my husband lost his job? There wasn't enough a me to go round. I wanted to scream at God, "How can you make me watch my child suffer so much? All I got to give her is a hug and a prayer and a few words." I woulda died for that child, but God didn't ast fer that. God just ast me to walk through it, with God by my side. As long as God never left me, that was enough. And God never left me.

I'm a-tellin' ya, sometimes this ole world is full a the most vile, cruel, nasty stuff. But Jesus has the lowdown on how to get through it. We got to take whatever we got and give it to him. And we got to trust that it'll be enough. It's not for me to say if you're gonna be like that boy with the biscuits and fish. You gonna have to decide. But if you been holdin' back on Jesus, don't think he don't know it. And if you been givin' yore dead level (very) best, he knows it.

But maybe you need some time to ast yourself if you are givin' all you can to Jesus. And if yore not, ast yousef, how many people did God feed with my little bit? Mabby you gonna be surprised whut can happen. Who'd a thought a little boy's lunch could feed so many people—with leftovers!

Celebration of Loaves and Fishes: A Mission Festival

The Celebration of Loaves and Fishes includes a one-hour worship service, an art display, mission displays, and a community meal. It can be done as part of a Sunday morning worship service or at a special time. The purposes are to:

- educate the congregation about the mission involvement of the church
- have an intergenerational event that celebrates the ministry of the church
- motivate people to give their time, money, and other gifts to benefit others
- show that whatever we give to Christ, he can multiply in ways that are beyond our imaginations!

Preparation:

At least three months prior to the event, organize the teams. One way to do this is to invite the youth to be the Hero Team and the children to be the Art Team. Adults and youth involved in mission can form the Display Team, and those who enjoy acting can be the Drama Team. The Worship Team includes musicians and worship leaders. Anyone who wants to help prepare the meal is put on the Stone Soup Team.

Teams:

- Worship Team: Plans the worship, including special music.
- Drama Team: Plans the dramatic presentation of "Mattie May: A Mountain Woman's Tale of a Gracious Plenty."
- Hero Team: Selects five people who demonstrate what one person can accomplish through vision, voice, and action. A "hero" is a person in the church, community, or world who is in service to others. Encourage the youth to identify people in the local community who have made a difference in the community, interview them, and write up their remarks about the qualities of the person and how they have helped others. Another approach is to relate the stories of the heroes in the book *Stone Soup for the World: Life-Changing Stories of Everyday Heroes.*[2]
- Art Team: Paint, draw or use any other medium to show what happened when the boy was willing to share his loaves and fishes (John 6:1-13). Select one to use as a bulletin cover or to put on a T-shirt for the event.

- Display Team(s): Learn about mission projects of the church and create a display, video, slides, or overhead projection to tell about the projects. A fellowship hall can be lined with tables that have a variety of displays, including youth mission trips, building teams, local soup kitchen helpers, or places that receive money given to missions.
- Stone Soup Team: Using the ingredients in the recipe in the back of the book *Stone Soup*[3], invite the congregation to bring something to contribute toward the community meal. The team gathers the ingredients and creates the soup and the rest of the meal.

Worship Bulletin
Order of Worship
(Designed for traditional worship but can be adapted to other styles.)

Prelude and Acolytes Bring Light to the Church

Opening Hymn: #67 "We, Thy People, Praise Thee" ***

Words of Welcome

Hymn: #405 "Seek Ye First" ***

Children's Moment

Read or tell the story of Stone Soup[4]. **Ask:** How did they have enough food at the end, when it seemed like they didn't have enough at the beginning? *(Everyone gave what they had, and together it was enough.)* What was the secret magic ingredient? *(Sharing. Prepare three children in advance to answer the question, "What do you think the world would be like if everyone gave whatever they had to help others?")*

Choral Call to Prayer #84 "Thank You, Lord" ***

Silent Prayer—Pastoral Prayer—The Lord's Prayer

Scripture Reading: John 6:1-13

Monologue: "Mattie May: A Mountain Woman's Tale of a Gracious Plenty"

Offering

* Doxology

Message: *(Suggested Titles: "The Power of One," "Is It Soup Yet?" "Soul Food," or "Soup's On!")*

Introduction: In the story of the stone soup, strangers arrived in tatters at a mountain village. They knocked on doors asking, "Do you care? Will you share? Do you have any food?" There are hometown heroes, everyday heroes, who have cared, shared, and made a difference. They do what they do, not to stand in the spotlight and get attention, but to help neighbors in need. Listen to the stories of five that have been selected to share with you. *(The Hero Team tells the stories of five heroes who have changed the world because they gave what they had. If the heroes are present, acknowledge them as a group. Invite the congregation to applaud what God has been doing in the lives of these people.)*

Closing: Our church's mission projects have been highlighted in a variety of displays in our building. We invite you to walk through the displays and give thanks to God for all of the people who are willing to give what they have to help their neighbors in need.

Closing Hymn: #389 "Freely, Freely"***

Taking Light to the World

* Benediction Response: #106 "God Is Able"***

* Choral Benediction: #99 "My Tribute"***
    Music Suggestions for Contemporary or Blended Worship Music:
    *#84 "The River Is Here"****
    *#43 "Hungry (Falling On My Knees)****
    *#54 "Let the River Flow"****

    #2126 "All Who Hunger"**
    #2139 "Oh, I Know the Lord's Laid His Hands On Me"**
    #2206 "Without Seeing You"**
    #2270 "He Has Made Me Glad"**
    #2258 "Sing Alleluia to the Lord"**

*** *** ***

Uses

- A Mission Festival: *Guide included.*
- Stewardship Sunday or Pledge Sunday.
- Midweek worship.
- Lenten study.

The Revised Common Lectionary
    Year B, Sunday between July 24 and 30 inclusive: John 6:1-21

---

*Congregation invited to stand.
**The Faith We Sing
***The United Methodist Hymnal
****Draw Me Close: 25 Top Vineyard Worship Songs

---

1. The Appalachian region extends from Maine to Alabama and includes parts of twelve states: Alabama, Georgia, Kentucky, Maryland, Ohio, New York, North Carolina, Pennsylvania, South Carolina, Tennessee, Virginia, and West Virginia. To hear a native mountain woman, listen to the selection entitled "Dellie Norton talks with Allen Tullos" on the CD that accompanies the book by Rom Amberg entitled *Sodom Laurel Album* (Chapel Hill: University of North Carolina Press in association with the Center for Documentary Studies, 2002). Selected photographs from the book can provide a glimpse into 1975 in the small mountain community of Sodom Laurel, North Carolina. The pictures can be used to introduce children to the mountain culture, but not all of the pictures are suitable for use with children. With permission from the publisher, the music on the CD can be used to create an awareness of the musical heritage of the region.
2. Marianne Larned, ed., *Stone Soup for the World: Life-Changing Stories of Everyday Heroes* (New York: Three Rivers Press, first published 1998, 2002).
3. Heather Forest, *Stone Soup* (Little Rock, Ark.: August House Little Folk, 1998).
4. Ibid.

CHAPTER 11

Bathsheba and King Dave: The Bigger the Ego, the Harder the Fall

By Karen Farish Miller

Editor's Note: This is a creative contemporary reading of the David and Bathsheba story. The leader should use this with specific audiences in mind.

Scripture: 2 Samuel 11:2–12:13; Psalm 51:1-14, Proverbs 16:18

Production options:

Minimal effort: Speaker stands at a podium or pulpit without any background or set and reads from the script. No props needed. Everyday clothing is worn.

Medium effort: Using gestures and facial expressions, one or more presenters pantomime all of the parts while one reader presents the monologue. Everyday clothes are worn or utilize the costume suggestions below.

Maximum effort: One reader and five nonspeaking persons: Bathsheba, King Dave, King's Assistant, Uriah, and the Storyteller.

Stage Setting: Use a backdrop, overhead projection, or scenery depicting a Middle Eastern palace. Any or all of the following can be added to the set: Oriental rug, large jewel tone pillows on the floor, table, chair, computer, large telescope, and greenery.

Props: Sunglasses, tanning lotion bottle, piece of paper with e-mail address: Bathsheba@mideast.com, cellular phone, mug, laptop computer, newspaper with the headline "Uriah the Hittite Killed in Battle," large suitcase and *The Message* Bible.

Alternate site for youth or young adults: Go to a skate park, bike park, trailhead, or mountain biking path, or just use these as themes. Example: Characters enter and exit on skateboards or bikes.

Costume: Choose from these options:
• Everyday clothing, with the king wearing a crown.
• Skateboarding, biking or hiking apparel. King Dave wears a cap or bandanna.
• Uriah wears a military uniform or camouflage clothing.
• A blend of everyday clothing and Old Testament costumes, such as jeans and T-shirt, worn with a Middle Eastern headpiece and sunglasses.

Presentation time: Six to 10 minutes.

Script placement: On a pulpit, podium, or the computer screen.

Script

Handsome King Dave is sitting on the roof of his high-rise palace gazing over the city through his telescope. *(Look through telescope and go past the target, then come back and pretend to focus the telescope with excited fascination.)* Suddenly, his lens lands on a woman sunbathing on the roof just below him.

(Look out at a distance, squint, look back through the telescope.) She's gorgeous with her sleek sunglasses and her string bikini. *(Put on sunglasses.)* She's lathering herself up with suntan lotion. *(Pour suntan lotion into hand and put some on. Remove sunglasses.)*

As King Dave watches, his heart races. Ba-boom, ba-boom, ba-boom! *(Gesture with hands beating over heart.).* He says to his assistant, "Find out who that is! She looks like she could be Miss Middle East. I want to know everything about her. Make sure you get her e-mail address."

The assistant returns saying, "Got what you wanted, Boss. But there's bad news. She couldn't be Miss Middle East. She'd have to run for Mrs. Middle East. She's married. Here's her e-mail address." *(Extend a piece of paper marked, Bathsheba@mideast.com.)*

King Dave writes, *(Type on laptop computer.)* "Dear Bathsheba, I saw you sunbathing on the roof. How would you like a tour of the royal palace? I'll show you things you've never seen before. Yours truly, King Dave." Her message comes back, *(Read from the computer screen.)* "Dear Dave, I'm a married woman. But I suppose a little peek at the palace couldn't hurt. See you at sixish. By the way, my husband, Uriah, is in your army. Maybe you know him. Sincerely, Bathsheba."

Bathsheba visits the palace and King Dave is infatuated with her. The next day he writes, *(Type on computer keyboard.)* "Dearest Bathshe-baby, I had a fabulous time last night. I can't get you out of my mind. Love, King Dave."

They continue e-mailing and visiting and a few weeks later she writes, "Dear Dave, Guess what! My pregnancy test was *(Pause.)* clear blue. I hope you'll like being Daddy Dave."

(Pacing.) King Dave paces the floor all night and finally decides that there is one way out of public humiliation and Bathsheba's husband finding out. If only he could get Uriah to think that HE was the father! But that would never happen as long as he was fighting at the front and never had any time to be with Bathsheba.

King Dave gets the head of Uriah's unit on the phone. *(Pick up a cell phone and dial some numbers. Speak into the phone.)* "This is King Dave. Yeah, you heard right. THE King Dave. I want you to give Uriah the Hittite a pass for the week. Yes. Just tell him he's needed at the palace. Thanks." *(Turn off the phone with a flourish.)*

Uriah shows up at the palace, saying, *(Stand straight and salute.)* "Uriah the Hittite, at your service, SIR!" *(End salute and click heels together.)*

King Dave puts his arm around Uriah and says, "Uriah, you've been out in the field too long. Go home, get cleaned up, and take it easy for a while. Take the whole week off. Spend some time with your wife. You need some R and R."

What King Dave was not banking on was that Uriah was Goody two-shoes of his army. Uriah says, *(Stand straight, salute, and say in a monotone military fashion.)*

"Your Royal Highness, SIR! It would be dishonorable for a soldier to return to his wife and enjoy the luxuries of home while the other soldiers are out in the field, SIR! I cannot betray you, O mighty King, SIR." *(End salute, click heels together.)*

As hard as King Dave tries, Uriah will not go home. Finally, King Dave throws a keg party. *(Pick up a mug.)* He thinks if he soaks Uriah's brain a little, he might go home . . . or he might think he did even if he didn't. Well, the party's almost over. King Dave and Uriah are sitting out on the porch. King Dave looks at Uriah and says, "I love ya, man."

And Uriah says, "That's cool . . . but I'm not going home." *(Put down the mug.)*

So, King Dave sends him back into the battle. He puts a call in to the head of Uriah's unit. *(Pick up cell phone. Dial some numbers. Speak into phone.)* Hello, this is King Dave. Yeah, THE King Dave. Here's what I want you to do. Put Uriah the Hittite front and center of the fighting. But that's not all. Pull out everyone else. Yes, that's right. *(Pause.)* I know, I know! Hey, I'm the king and I give the orders. *(Pause.)* Right. *(Pause.)* Okay. Let me know what happens, but I've got a pretty good idea. Just do it! *(End phone call.)*

(Newspaper is thrown on stage.) The word comes back to the palace that *(Open and read the newspaper headline, show the audience the words, "Uriah the Hittite is Killed in Battle.")* Uriah is killed in battle! *(Use facial expressions of disbelief.)* King Dave e-mails Bathsheba his condolences. *(Type on laptop.)* "Dear Bathsheba. I know you must be grieving the loss of such a *(Pause and think.)* good and honest man. He was a true hero. Why don't you come to the palace so that I can comfort and console you? Sharing your sadness, King Dave." *(Smile.)*

Bathsheba writes back, *(Read from computer screen.)* "Thanks for the kind words. I'll be there by dinnertime. Love, Bathsheba."

Bathsheba moves in with King Dave. *(She drags a suitcase across the stage area. Bathsheba and King Dave sit and listen to the storyteller.)* A few days later the king invites a storyteller to provide after dinner entertainment. The storyteller says, "There was a fellow who had a lamb. The man raised the lamb since it was a baby, feeding her with a baby bottle, letting her come into the house. She had soft eyes that made everyone melt who gazed upon the fair creature. This fellow treated that lamb like a member of his family.

"A circus came to town with all kinds of animals, including camels like the ones you've got out there, *(Point with thumb.)* and lions and tigers and bears, oh my! *(Ask the audience to repeat the phrase "lions, and tigers and bears, oh my!" several times.)*

"This circus had every animal imaginable. But the circus lamb got sick and died. The owner of the circus heard about this man who raised a lamb, and he wanted it. It didn't matter that he had any other animal he could ever want in the circus. He wanted that lamb. So he went out in the middle of the night and stole the lamb. Just loaded it on a truck and took off."

King Dave is engrossed in the story. "No way! I would cut his head off. I would have him executed without a blindfold. Who could be that cruel?"

The storyteller looks him straight in the eye and says, "You the man."

King Dave says, "I haven't stolen a lamb."

The storyteller says, "No, you've stolen Uriah's wife and put a contract out on Uriah. You've heard of God's ten big ones, including not coveting your neighbor's wife, not committing adultery, not murdering anyone. You're in deep . . . well, deep trouble."

"God, what am I going to do?" cries King Dave.

The storyteller says, "At least you're starting at the right place. It's God you've hurt by what you've done. And Bathsheba. And, of course, Uriah and yourself. What you've got to do is confess your sin and let God take care of your messed up life."

King Dave feels lower than an earthworm. So he goes into his temple and this is what he cries to God. *(Read from The Message, Psalm 51:1-14.)*

Worship

Praise and Worship Service

Song: "Come, Now Is the Time To Worship"[1]

Words of Welcome and Announcements: Provide prayer cards to fill in prayer concerns and joys. Participants come forward and put them in a prayer bowl.

Praise Reports and Testimonies: Participants stand and share the ways that they have seen God at work this week.

Prayer and Lord's Prayer

Praise and Worship Songs:
    #2070 " He Is Exalted"**
    #2071 "Jesus, Name Above All Names"**
    #2064 "O Lord, You're Beautiful"**
    #2039 "Holy, Holy"**

Scripture Reading: 2 Samuel 11:2–12:13 *(Either of the following can be used throughout the service: Psalm 51:1-14, Proverbs 16:18.)*

Drama: "Bathsheba and King Dave: The Bigger the Ego, the Harder the Fall"

Offering

    Music: "I Stand Amazed"[2]

Sermon: *(Suggested Titles: "When the Only Place Left to Fall Is On Your Knees," "If You Don't Stand for Anything, You'll Fall for Everything," "How Do You Spell Relief?" (The answer revealed in the sermon is F-O-R-G-I-V-E-N.)*

Video Clip: *The Mission*[3] (Obtain any necessary permissions.)
    Introduce the video: The story takes place on the borderlands of Argentina, Brazil, and Paraguay in 1750. The historical events represented in the story are true. Rodrigo Mendosa, played by Robert De Niro, traps Indians and sells them as slaves. In the first part of the movie, Mendosa is spurned by a woman he cares for because she loves his brother. Enraged, Mendosa kills his brother in a sword fight.

In the scene you are about to see, Mendosa has given up on life because of his guilt and shame over killing his brother. Father Gabriel, played by actor Jeremy Irons, is a Spanish Jesuit priest sent to help him. Father Gabriel speaks to Mendosa about redemption. When Mendosa scorns redemption, Father Gabriel asks if he has the courage to choose his own penance. (Penance is a belief that by performing some service or punishment, God provides a way out of sin.) In this clip, Mendosa carries a huge burden as penance because he cannot accept God's love and forgiveness. Watch what happens.

Reflection: Praise team sings softly: #2152 "Change My Heart, O God"** or #2193 "Lord, Listen to Your Children Praying"**

(Ask people to think about what has been said and pray in place or pray at the kneeling rail.)

Song: #69 "Refiner's Fire"**** or #2131 "Humble Thyself in the Sight of the Lord"**

* Benediction: **"May your life be guided by The Way of Love."** (Read aloud 1 Corinthians 13:4-7 from *The Message*.)

* Closing Song: #2284 "Joy in the Morning"**
    Alternate music suggestions:
        #707 "Hymn of Promise"***
        #365 "Grace Greater than Our Sin"***
        #383 "This Is a Day of New Beginnings"***

***

High School Youth or Young Adult Bible Study

• Use slides, video, or photos of a bike or skateboard competition. Show one slide of a biker or skater with this paraphrase of Proverbs 16:18, "First pride, then the crash—the bigger the ego, the harder the fall" (*The Message*). Then present the dramatization.

Talking Points

1. Some people get a rush from seeing how close they can come to the edge of death or injury without getting hurt. Those who are successful are rewarded with the applause of the crowd, the approval of friends, and the celebration party. The rush causes enthusiasts to try newer and harder stunts that have a higher degree of risk. Can you name a celebrity who engages in stunts with a high degree of risk?

2. Gravity is a natural law that governs such sports. As many times as you try to defeat it or go against it, gravity will always win. Why? What goes up, must come down. God made it that way. What are some of the sports that seem to challenge gravity? (*Water or snow skiing, biking, skateboarding, parachuting.*)

3. Just as God created the law of gravity, God has intentions about the way humans relate to one another. People are to be cared about and treated with dignity and respect. This is just as binding as the law of gravity. Have you ever known someone who *used* another person for their own enjoyment, without really caring about the needs or feelings of the other person? Have you ever felt used by another person?

4. King Dave used Bathsheba for his own pleasure without respect for her marriage or her dignity. His risky behavior had dangerous consequences. What were some of them? *(It destroyed her marriage, caused the death of her husband, and caused both King Dave and Bathsheba to sin.)*

5. When a person attempts to defy the law of gravity, there are often painful consequences. What do you think might be three consequences when a person uses another person without respecting his or her feelings? Has this ever happened to you?

6. State whether you agree or disagree with the following sentence and the reasons why. "Since King Dave was more powerful than Bathsheba, he was more at fault than she was." *(One form of sexual harassment is a person in power using that power to take advantage of another person. Dave's position as king meant that women in his kingdom would have a conflict between their desire to please their king and their desire to be true to their marriage and beliefs. They were particularly vulnerable to his advances. This allowed Dave to take unfair advantage of Bathsheba. A king should live by a high standard of responsibility. Instead, he used his role as king to steal another man's wife and have him killed.)*

7. When King Dave realized that he had done something wrong, his response was to offer a prayer of confession. Look at the passage in Psalm 51 and outline the way that David confessed.
   a. Asking for God's help (verses 1-2)
   b. Admitting that he sinned against God, remembering God's delight in honesty (verses 3-6)
   c. Asking for forgiveness and cleansing (verses 5-6, 10)
   d. Receiving God's gift of forgiveness

8. 1 John 1:9 describes God's response to a prayer of confession. ("If we confess our sins, he who is faithful and just will forgive us our sins and cleanse us from all unrighteousness.") God is eager to forgive us when we've done something wrong. Why? *(God loves us.)*

9. Hand out pencils and paper for students to write down the names of anyone that they have related to recently in a way that would not be pleasing to God.

10. Provide five to ten minutes to use the steps outlined under number 7 to write or pray a prayer of repentance.

11. Discuss how to make things right with the person or persons the student wrote down, such as going to talk with them, telling the person what was done that was wrong, and asking for forgiveness.

12. On a scale of 1 to 10, with 10 being the most difficult, how difficult is it for you to forgive yourself when you have hurt another person? Read John 12:24-26. Discuss what it means when Jesus says that a grain of wheat must die and be buried to produce fruit. This passage is about yielding yourself to God so that you can start over. What do you need to do in your own life to forgive yourself for mistakes you have made and start over? Listen or sing "Give Me a New Heart"[4] or "On My Knees."[5]

***

Uses

- Praise and worship, contemporary or blended service: *Worship Outline included.*
- Youth or young adult worship or Bible study: *Talking Points included.*
- Camp, retreat, or other group setting.
- Watch Night on New Year's Eve.
- Ash Wednesday.
- Youth or adult retreat.
- Not recommended for traditional worship.

The Revised Common Lectionary
    Year B, Sunday between July 24 and 30 inclusive: 2 Samuel 11:1-15
    Year B, Sunday between July 31 and August 6 inclusive: 2 Samuel 11:26–12:13*a*
    Year B, Sunday between July 31 and August 6 inclusive: Psalm 51:1-12

*Congregation invited to stand.
**The Faith We Sing
***The United Methodist Hymnal
****Draw Me Close: 25 Top Vineyard Worship Songs

---

1. "Come Now Is the Time to Worship." *WOW Worship Yellow 2003 Songbook or CD*. Franklin, Tenn.: Brentwood-Benson Music Publishing, Inc., 2003. Performed by Phillips, Craig and Dean on *WOW Worship* Yellow CD.
2. "I Stand Amazed." *WOW Worship Yellow 2003 Songbook or CD*. Performed by GlassByrd on *WOW Worship* Yellow CD.
3. *The Mission*, written by Robert Bolt and directed by Roland Joffe, Warner Communications Company, an Enigma Production in Association with Fernando Ghia. The film won two awards at the 1986 Cannes Film Festival, the year it was released. Start the clip at 26.37 when Father Gabriel offers Lorenzo a bowl of food in jail. End the clip at 40.29, when Lorenzo weeps. Shorten or edit the clip to remove shots of the Indians' partial nudity or prepare the audience in advance. Some viewers may be offended by the Native American attire and will not be able to focus on the clip.
4. "Give Me A New Heart," written and performed by John Wyrosdick on *My Redeemer Lives* album. Vineyard Music Group, 1996.
5. "On My Knees" performed by Jaci Velasquez on *Heavenly Place* CD. Sony, 1996.

CHAPTER 12

Esther: Chosen for Such a Time as This

By Karen Farish Miller

Scripture: The Book of Esther

Stage setting: None needed.
Costume:
   Minimal effort: Everyday clothing
   Medium effort: Simple robe or sari; tiara or crown.
Presentation time: Nine to ten minutes.
Script placement: Behind a large fan or scroll.

Script

My name is Esther. Both of my parents died when I was too young to remember, so I lived with the family of my cousin Mordecai. He adopted me and was as loving and good as any father. Our village was part of a vast kingdom from India to Ethiopia that was ruled by King Ahasuerus. In our village we heard that the king had thrown a magnificent party that lasted for a week.

At the end of the week, the king summoned Queen Vashti to show her to his friends, for she was very beautiful. But Queen Vashti refused to come. The king was enraged that she would not follow his command, and he banished her from the palace.

(Walking slowly across the stage and reading from a scroll.) A decree was sent throughout the kingdom that women must honor their husbands. The king appointed officers in all of the provinces of the kingdom to gather the beautiful virgins to his harem, that he might select a new queen who would please him.

I went fearfully with the other maidens to the capital city. We had to go. It was the edict of the king. But I longed for my simple way of life with my Hebrew family.

All of the young women spent a year preparing for our appearance before the king. For six months we applied oil of myrrh to our skin and hair, *(Gesture as if applying lotion to face.)* and for six months we applied spices and ointments, so the king would find us beautiful.

(Place fist on chest.) My heart pounded when I went before King Ahasuerus. I stood tall, *(Standing straight.)* but not so tall as to appear too proud or too bold. The king

saw all of the women who had been gathered together from the kingdom, but he chose me to have the highest place a woman could have in the kingdom. He did not know that I was Hebrew, for Mordecai had charged me not to make it known. I was trembling as the king placed the royal crown on my head. *(Place tiara or crown on head.)*

The king gave a great banquet for all his princes and servants, calling it Esther's banquet. He even granted remission of taxes to the provinces and gave many gifts. About that time, Mordecai was sitting at the king's gate. He overheard two of the king's guards talking about assassinating King Ahasuerus. Mordecai sent word to me, and I had the matter investigated. As a result, the two guards were hanged on the gallows.

The king promoted a man named Haman to be over all of the princes. All of the king's servants bowed down to Haman, *(Bends over from the waist, facing the floor.)* for the king commanded that they must. But when Haman passed Mordecai, he would not bow down. *(Stands up straight.)* As a Jew, Mordecai would only pay homage to God, not to any man. This filled Haman with fury.

Haman's friends told him Mordecai was a Jew, so Haman schemed to destroy all the Jews in the kingdom. Haman approached the king slyly, describing our people as disrespectful to the king's laws. He convinced the king that our people should be destroyed. An edict was signed with the imprint of the king's ring, *(Gesture the imprinting of a ring by making a fist and turning hand upside down.)* indicating that the edict could not be revoked.

I felt as if the world would end when I heard that my people would be murdered and their goods plundered. *(Put hands over ears, facial expression showing horror. Shake head in disbelief.)* There seemed to be nothing I could do to stop the edict. The documents were sent out, and all I could do was cry many tears. In eleven months my people would be destroyed. *(Pause.)*

A servant told me that when Mordecai heard about the edict, he was so overcome with grief that he went out in the midst of the city, wailing with a loud and bitter cry. He tore his clothes and put on sackcloth and ashes. Everywhere the king's edict was made known there was great mourning and weeping.

I sent garments to Mordecai, but he wouldn't accept them. He told my messenger that Haman had promised to pay a large sum of money into the king's treasuries for the destruction of the Jews. He asked me to go to the king and intercede for my people.

I knew that no one went into the inner court of the king without being called, not a man, and certainly not a woman. All alike are put to death unless the king holds out the golden scepter when the person approaches. The king had not called me to come into his court for thirty days. I sent this word to Mordecai, fearing that the king would take my life if I spoke in behalf of my people.

Mordecai sent this message back: "Do not think that just because you are in the king's palace, you will escape anymore than any other Jew. If you keep silent now, relief for the Jews will come from somewhere, but you will perish. And who knows whether you have not come to the kingdom for such a time as this?"

I knew what I had to do. I sent word to Mordecai to gather the Jews together to fast on my behalf for three days, and Mordecai did as I asked. I fasted to prepare myself.

I anointed my body with oils and spices and put on my royal robe. I walked into the inner court of the king's palace, opposite the king's hall. The king was sitting on the throne. When our eyes met, he seemed surprised. For one terrifying moment we looked at one another, then he held out the golden scepter that was in his hand. *(Pantomime extending the scepter.)* I approached and touched the top of the scepter.

The king smiled and said, "What is it, Queen Esther? What is your request? I will give you as you desire, even to half of the kingdom."

I said, "Let the king and Haman come this day to a dinner that I have prepared." He hurriedly called Haman, and we went to dinner. I wanted to make sure that I had found favor in the eyes of the king, so I invited him to dine with me again the next day, with Haman present again. The king was delighted, promising me the desires of my heart. I wondered if he would feel so joyful when he heard what I had to say.

Haman ran home to gloat to his wife that he had been invited to dine at our banquet table. He still burned with anger that Mordecai would not bow down and pay homage to him as the other men did. He consulted his wife and friends and decided to hang Mordecai the next day. If he had his way, Mordecai would be hanged before we dined again.

The king was restless that night and called for the Book of Memorable Deeds. When he read of Mordecai's heroic act that saved the king from assassination, he called his servant and asked if anything had been done to reward Mordecai for this act. Just as he found out that Mordecai had not been rewarded, Haman appeared in the outer courtyard. The king asked Haman, "What should be done to the man whom the king delights to honor?"

Haman thought the king was talking about himself. Delighted at this prospect, he suggested that the man be dressed in royal robes. *(Sweep hand in front of body.)* Haman said the man also should be put on a horse that the king had ridden and be brought through the square with the proclamation, "This is how the king honors a man."

The king was pleased. He asked Haman to take the robes and the horse to Mordecai and parade him through the town crying out, "This is how the king honors a man." Haman followed the king's command *(Speak slowly.)* but went home ashamed with his head covered.

Soon it came time for the banquet that I had prepared for the king and Haman. The king asked me to name my request. I knew the time had come to speak what was on my heart. "Let my life be spared and the lives of my people. We are to be sold, destroyed, and slain because of the actions of one man." I waited to see the king's reaction. He asked the name of the man who would do this. I looked directly at Haman and said, "A foe and an enemy. This wicked Haman!"

(Speaking quickly.) The king fled angrily to the garden. He left me alone with Haman, who began to beg for his life. When the king returned, Haman was attacking me on the couch. The king was enraged. *(Loudly.)* He said, "Will he even assault the queen in my presence, in my own palace?" That very day, the king hanged Haman on the gallows Haman had built as a place for Mordecai to die. *(Pause and move slowly across the stage.)*

Now the king knew that I was a Jew. He knew that Mordecai was my cousin, and he invited him to head the house of Haman. The king was generous, but my heart was still unsettled about Haman's plot to destroy the Jews. Nothing had been done to reverse the edict. I fell at the king's feet and cried for him to avert Haman's evil plan. He turned to Mordecai and said, "I have given Esther the house of Haman, and he has been hanged on the gallows because he would lay hands on the Jews. You may write as you please with regard to the Jews in my name and seal it with my ring."

Although the king's edict could not be lifted, the Jews were allowed to gather and defend themselves. There was great joy and gladness among the Jews, and we celebrated with a feast and a holiday.

Mordecai became great in the house of the king. The former enemies of the Jews feared that if they laid a hand on a Jew, Mordecai would deal with them vengefully. Then the Jews became powerful, slaying their enemies with the sword. There was great celebration when our foes were slain. The festival of Purim was set aside so that every year the day would be remembered as a time when our sorrow was turned into gladness, our mourning turned into a holiday.

Mordecai became next in rank to the king himself, and he was great among the Jews and popular with the multitude. I am grateful that I had come to the kingdom for such a time as this and that the Lord saved my people from destruction through me.

Women's Conference

Schedule

8:00 – 8:45	Registration with coffee and refreshments
8:45 – 9:00	Words of Welcome and Music
9:00 – 9:45	"Esther's Story and Our Story" (Session 1)
9:45 – 10:30	Break and Music
10:30 – 11:45	"For Such A Time As This!" (Session 2)
11:45 – 11:55	Break
11:55 – 1:00	Blessing and Lunch
1:00 – 1:15	Music
1:15 – 2:15	"Stumbling Blocks or Stepping-Stones?" (Session 3)
2:15 – 2:30	Prayer

Leadership Teams

- Prayer team
- Facilities
- Registration brochures
- Flyers and press release
- Registration table
- Name tags
- Snacks
- Conference decorations
- Luncheon committee

- Planning team
- Servers
- Hostesses

For Such a Time As This!

When participants arrive, each is provided a folder containing the handouts found at the end of this chapter, music, a list thanking the speaker and those who served on leadership teams, copyright information for additional texts, license information for copyrighted music, and a statement crediting the publisher and author for the material used from this chapter. Additionally, the words to the music (with any necessary permissions granted) and the four handouts may be projected on an overhead screen.

Opening Music:
#578 "God of Love and God of Power"***
#2032 "My Life Is In You, Lord"**

Welcome
Welcome to this special time set aside for women who desire to open their lives to God. By studying the story of Esther, we will learn to use our individual and collective resources for God. Let us open our hearts and minds to the power of God as we pray together.

Opening Prayer
We offer ourselves and our time to you, God. We ask you to speak to us and through us, that we may experience you more deeply and hear your voice more clearly. Help us leave behind other cares that we might be fully present to each other and to the insights you want to bring to us. We pray for your power to transform us, that we might be a part of your transformation of the world. In the name of Christ we pray. Amen.

Introductions
Let's start by getting to know the women around your table. Please tell your name to a partner, and then tell something about your name, such as whom you are named for, the ethnic origin of your name, a nickname, or whatever you would like to share. Then your partner will introduce you to others at your table and tell something about your name.

Session 1: Esther's Story and Our Story
The Old Testament book of Esther can be found in two forms today. The shortest form is in the Hebrew Bible. The Greek Bible has 107 verses that the Hebrew does not have, and this makes the story much more interesting. This longer reading is found in *The New Jerusalem Bible*. It is beautifully written, and today we will share the basic plot. To get the full impact of the book, you must read it yourself.

Monologue: "Esther: Chosen for Such a Time as This"

(The monologue may be presented by the retreat leader or by another person.)
Say: Have there been times in your life when everything seemed to stand still, times when everything seems to revolve around you in a grand way? For Esther, it happened when she was crowned queen, and everyone celebrated her at Esther's banquet.

(Use a personal illustration of a special time you can remember such as prom night. Describe how the formal gown, the perfect corsage, the high heels, and the trip to the beauty salon all make a girl feel very special.)

At weddings, graduations, anniversary celebrations, even the day her baby takes that first step, a woman can have a sense of being suspended in a moment when everything is sweeter than she can stand, and life is good.

We have other special kinds of time. *(Choose a personal illustration, such as being pregnant and feeling a baby kick the first time, when you felt called to ordained ministry, or when you were selected or elected for something.)*

As great as that banquet celebration must have been for Esther, she had an equally horrible moment later when she felt like her world was crumbling beneath her feet. Her people were to be killed, and she didn't feel she had the power to do anything about it.

We all face death-like moments if we live long enough. We have times when it seems like every ounce of energy we have is squeezed out of us. Sometimes we give ourselves for some person other than ourselves. Husband, children, work, church, friends all require our attention. Sometimes it seems like nothing in our lives is our own, and there is very little, or nothing, given back to us in return. The toddler follows us everywhere, even into the bathroom. Or the aging relative requires around-the-clock attention, and all our effort is poured into providing care.

We have times when we worry. The doctor says there's something abnormal about the Pap smear or the mammogram. The teenager misses curfew again. The bills are piling up, and the paycheck won't stretch any further.

As women we have times when we feel that we have a place and other times when we cannot find our place. Sometimes we don't know where we belong. We can't find Mr. Right. We can't figure out what kind of work suits us. We feel lonely even when we are with people. It just doesn't seem like we have found our place. *(Give a personal illustration.)*

We have times when life seems harsh and brutal. We have wilderness times, when we doubt God and ourselves, and everybody else better stay out of our way. We may want to lock all of the doors and pull the covers up over our heads.

Sometimes we don't realize the kind of time we're in while we are in it.

(Illustrations: *Stone Soup For the World*[1] pp.197-199, 357-360)

The life of a woman is filled with all kinds of times. What kind of time is this for you? The first handout will help you identify what kind of time it is in your life. Take a few moments to fill this out. When you have finished, share the most important thing in each quadrant with a partner. When you have completed this, you may take a break. After the break, we will talk about how to be empowered by our faith for this time in your life.

(Participants fill out HANDOUT #1: WHAT KIND OF TIME IS THIS?)

Break

While participants are returning to the room, sing favorite songs or select from the list below.

#632 "Draw Us in the Spirit's Tether"***

#601 "Thy Word Is a Lamp"***

#2214 "Lead Me, Guide Me"**

#2163 "He Who Began a Good Work in You"**

Session 2: "For Such a Time as This"

Esther realized that she had come to the kingdom for a reason. She was afraid that she would lose her life if she went into the presence of the king without his calling her. Mordecai had to convince her that the lives of many people were at stake and that she could make a difference.

Mordecai sent word to Esther, "Do not suppose that, because you are in the king's palace, you are going to be the one Jew to escape. No; if you persist in remaining silent at such a time, relief and deliverance will come to the Jews from another quarter, but both you and your father's whole family will perish. Who knows? Perhaps you have come to the throne for just such a time as this" (Esther 4:12-14 NJB).

Esther thought, "I am here in this palace, nothing can happen to me here." She believed she was safe and protected. Mordecai knew differently. He knew she was uniquely placed where she could intervene for the Jewish people. What kind of power does God want us to have? The power that God gives is not for privilege, but to be used for Christ and others.

What does being part of the church mean to you? Sometimes we need the church to be a safe place to go when all of the world is clamoring around us. Other times we need the church to be a place where we can worship God and walk away refreshed. Mothers may enjoy having one day to be able to trust someone else to look after young children, so they can worship and relax!

As hectic as our lives can be at times, it is tempting to see the church only for what it can give us or do for us. But if we look at it that way, we understand only part of what the church is. The story of Esther shows us that there are times when difficult decision-making and risk are required if we are going to accomplish what God wants us to do. Esther had to get to the place where she was ready to die for her people. Remember her words, "If I perish, I perish" (Esther 4:17 NJB). Perhaps being a part of a church is much more risky than we ever understood!

Consider what happened to Jesus when he faced the possibility of persecution and death. He knelt and prayed, "My Father, if it is possible, let this cup pass from me; yet not what I want but what you want"(Matthew 26:39 NRSV). We all would like to avoid difficult situations and just enjoy our faith. Esther encourages us to do more than enjoy our faith. We are to be empowered by our faith.

(Illustration: *Stone Soup for the World*[2], pp. 18-20.)

Some of us may be afraid to see the ways that we can change or enact change. We don't even like to change where we sit in worship on Sunday, much less make a big change. So how do we prepare for change? Let's look at the handout.

(Have participants look at HANDOUT #2: PREPARATION FOR CHANGE.
Add your personal comments or illustrations to the list, building
on the scripture passages listed.)

Seeing clearly how something can be better. We can't begin to institute change if we don't believe something can be improved upon. Sometimes we have to feel a sense of discontentment before we are motivated to change. In Esther 4:14, Mordecai sent word to Esther that she was in the kingdom to use her power to help her people.

Seeing the importance of making a change. Examine the consequences of making or not making a change. If the consequence is important, it is worth all of the effort. Esther 4:10-11 shows that Esther had not been willing to risk her life by going before the king. Mordecai had to convince her that the results were worth the risk.

Realizing that you can make a difference. You have to believe in yourself or no one else will. Compare Esther 4:4-11 to Esther 5:1-3. Esther's distress about the destruction of the Jews was transformed into action when she realized she could make a difference.

Knowing how to do it. If you can't see how to make the change, ask yourself who might help you. What resources, relationships, or roles can you use to make the needed change? Esther 4:15-16 shows Esther's plan was to gather the support of the Jews and then to go before the king to ask for the freedom of her people.

Seeking support from others. This applies not only to the obvious tasks that the change will entail but also the spiritual support of prayer and fasting. Esther 4:16 shows that Esther asked the Jews to fast and that she and her maids fasted. She was able to rally the strength of many others besides herself. Through their common strength, she had the power to step forward and take the necessary risk.

Esther discovered her purpose and then used all of her ability to accomplish what she set out to do. What is OUR purpose? Perhaps it is to be bold in the face of conflict, to confront the forces that oppose God's will in this world even when it is fearful and difficult for us. How can we gain the courage that we need to have this boldness? We must be filled to overflowing with the spirit of Christ.

(Using a pitcher, fill a cup or chalice all the way to the top with water and place it in a large bowl. As you talk about the relationships, events, and demands on a woman's life, gradually pour more water from the pitcher into the cup or chalice. When the cup runs over, say that you cannot put in one more drop until something is poured out. One of the reasons that we cannot put Christ into our lives is that our lives are too full of other things to have room for him. We need to make room for him in our lives.)

Take some time as we close this session to ask yourself, "What do I need to do to empty myself out so that there is room for Christ?" *(During ten minutes of quiet time, provide art supplies for this to be depicted in a variety of ways—drawing, painting, making a collage out of magazine clippings, or writing poetry. Encourage those who are willing to share their work to display their work on the walls or tables around the room.)*

Blessing

Holy God, we thank you for the gift of food when we are hungry and drink when we are thirsty. As you quench our hunger and thirst with the meal that has been provided, also quench our hunger for fellowship and friendship by helping us get to know the people who are sharing this day with us. Thank you for providing everything that we truly need. In the name of Christ Jesus we pray. Amen.

Lunch

Music: Select any of the following for group singing, or presentation by a choral group or soloist.

#585 "This Little Light of Mine"***
#584 "Lord, You Give the Great Commission"***
#581 "Lord, Whose Love Through Humble Service"***
#572 "Pass It On"***
#560 "Help Us Accept Each Other"***

#2164 "Sanctuary"**
#2208 "Guide My Feet"**
#2244 "People Need the Lord"**
#2203 "In His Time"**
#2146 "His Eye Is on the Sparrow"**

#20 "Cry of My Heart"****
#61 "Lord Reign In Me"****
#66 "More Love More Power"****

Session 3: Stumbling Blocks or Stepping-Stones?

Do you know what a stepping-stone is? Did you ever go to a creek or a swimming hole where there was no bridge and no way to cross the water except to find the stones sticking up out of the water? You could step from one rock to the other all the way across the creek. Stepping-stones help you get where you are going. *(Give personal illustration.)*

What do you know about stumbling blocks? You may have found yourself walking along a sidewalk or stair step and a child has left something in your way. You put your foot down on it or kick it, and you fall down to the ground. A stumbling block is something that you can't anticipate, something that you can't get around. *(Give personal illustration.)*

All kinds of events happen to us in a lifetime. We have the right to interpret these events any way we choose. Sometimes we think of things as stumbling blocks that stand in our way and cause us terrible pain. But a stumbling block could be a stepping-stone.

(Illustration: *Stone Soup For the World*[3], pp. 345-349.)

Esther was queen in a country where all of her people, the Jews, were to be killed. Her cousin Mordecai realized the terrible attack that was about to happen. He began weeping and wailing. He put on sackcloth and ashes. Esther's first response to Mordecai was not to consider, "I wonder what I can do to change this situation since I am in a place of power?" She sent Mordecai a change of clothes. She was treating the symptom, not the cause.

When Mordecai asked her to help her people, she became concerned about one thing. Herself. She was afraid that if she went to the king on behalf of the Jews, she would fall out of favor with him, and she might be killed. Fear was motivating her.

Mordecai was able to pull Esther back to her senses when he said, "Perhaps you have come to the throne for just such a time as this!" (Esther 4:14 NJB). Esther's perspective changed. She saw the opportunity, the stepping-stone, before her. She was willing to adopt a new attitude. She said, "If I perish, I perish"(Esther 4:17 NJB). She surrendered concern for herself for a larger concern.

The next step was preparing herself for what she had to do. She planned her strategy. She used all the resources that she had. She made herself beautiful to appeal to the king. She also fasted and asked others to fast. Then she invited Haman and the king to dinner twice. Once she was in the king's good graces, she told him about Haman's evil plan against the Jews.

Let's look at what some of the stumbling blocks can be for us.

(Ask participants to look at HANDOUT #3: STUMBLING BLOCKS. Invite them to add other stumbling blocks to the list. Using your own life experiences, lead them to consider how God can turn a stumbling block into a stepping-stone.)

Let's use an action plan to see how we might respond to the various times of our lives. *(You may use the suggestions below or create some of your own.)*

(Ask participants to look at HANDOUT #4: ACTION PLAN. State the questions listed on the plan.)

First let's look at a family issue.

Imagine that your last or only son or daughter is moving away from home. Although you want to be able to release your child, difficult issues of letting go are prominent at this time in your life.

1. What are the stumbling blocks? *(Wait for a member of the group to answer. Some of the answers that might emerge follow.)* You are struggling to break the emotional ties that you have to this person you brought into the world. You feel the urgent need to explain to your emerging young adult everything about life that you don't think they understand. You are anxious about what might happen when you no longer have the kind of influence you had when the young person was under your roof. You find yourself looking at baby pictures and crying. You are knocking heads with your young person who desperately wants to be treated like an emerging adult, not a child.

2. What action steps are you going to follow? *(Listen to the answers that come from the group, then add any of these that are not listed.)* You could talk with another mother who has been through this transition and find out how she coped. She may be able to explain and affirm the complex family dynamics at work. You might write a letter that says the things you hoped to say to your son or daughter. You may want to put together a scrapbook or memory book to claim the blessings of your life together. For some, it may mean that with your teenager out of the house, you now have time to take a class, engage in a hobby, or volunteer your time in ways that you were not able to do in the past. Find a new way to develop yourself.

3. Where are you going to start? *(Let the group talk about what to do right now.)* Call that friend today. Write the letter to your son or daughter before the week is out. Create that scrapbook at the kitchen table today.

Let's make an action plan for a work-related concern.

The issue is that you have a coworker who appears hospitable to you but talks about you in critical and demeaning ways when you are not around. Your professional reputation has taken some hits because this coworker degrades you to your boss and other colleagues. Recently there has been a situation where you were publicly humiliated by this coworker.

1. What are some stumbling blocks you might encounter? *(Give the group time to answer.)* Your approach to this situation could be a stumbling block. You've avoided talking directly to the complaining coworker. By ignoring the remarks and hoping they will go away, the problem has only gotten worse. You are thinking about quitting your job without working through the issue. A stumbling block can be the lack of courage to take an active part in changing the situation.

2. Let's talk about action steps. *(Ask the group to suggest steps.)* Some of the possible options might be to talk with your boss or supervisor but that would create a triangle that might not be healthy. What do you think would happen if you spoke directly to the coworker about your concerns? Or if you attempted to discover the reasons for his or her behavior? What options do you think might be the most effective?

3. Now you have a plan, but how are you going to get started and when? What is the first thing you would do in this case? It might be to bring this up in the next conversation you have alone with the coworker. Or go to your superior and ask for assistance. Taking the next step and taking control of your situation will help you "in such a time as this."

Let's look at a community issue and create an action plan.
You are very concerned about the growing number of women who are homeless in your community. You have met a few of them as you volunteered in the shelter, which had formerly been primarily for males. The vulnerability and desperation you have seen on their faces causes you to want to do something to provide a better living situation for them. But you don't know what to do.

1. What is a stumbling block to making a positive change in your community? *(Let the group make suggestions.)* Perhaps the most common stumbling block is to do nothing. Many community issues seem so overwhelming that we mentally shift the responsibility to someone else. We may not know who to link up with to find solutions. We may fear getting criticized if we make bold statements, propose changes, or get personally involved. We may think we do not have the time or resources to make a difference.

2. What is a possible action plan to help homeless women? *(Listen to the responses to the group.)* One place to start would be to find out what other communities have done. An Internet search may give ideas. Talk with community groups to see what types of shelters or low income housing are available, and what it would take to help a woman find a way to get off the streets. Find others who share your concern. Demonstrate the need to your church or other caring agency. Then pick a plan, such as "Room in the Inn," a program in which churches house and feed homeless people two or three weeks a year. Volunteers stay in the church for a night to provide a safe, home-like environment. Church volunteers provide the food.[4]

3. What would be the first steps to begin a "Room in the Inn" program in your community? *(Wait for their answer.)* You could begin by picking up your phone, making a contact with a community leader, or looking for ideas on the Internet.

Let's look at an issue related to self and see what action might be needed
Let's say that this is a time when life is too full. You need some Sabbath moments. That is, you need some spiritual rest that allows you to be attentive to God. You need to plan how you will do it.

1. The stumbling block is that if you do it first thing when you get up, you will be rushed for the rest of the morning. If you do it the last thing in the day, you'll fall asleep.

2. So, what do you need to plan in order to have a quiet, focused time with God? That is the action needed. *(Ask for their response.)*

3. Can you make time in the afternoon with a quiet devotional time while the children are napping? Or perhaps when you are at work, you can take a walk outside during lunch and let your mind clear. Perhaps you need to take some vacation days just to be alone.

Now that we have learned how to create an action plan, let's work together to create some action plans together using the first handout. *(For each of the situations they suggest, listen, then solicit participants' suggestions about stumbling blocks, possible actions, and what to do when.)*

1. What is something in the area of work or self that someone needs to change?
2. Is there an important community concern that you have listed?
3. What is a work-related issue?

Now that we have worked through some of these together, it's time for you to tackle the concerns in your own life. Choose any of the issues in the circle in the first handout and create your own action plan. You will have a chance to share these later with one or two others from your table.

(Ask participants to complete HANDOUT #4 ACTION PLAN.)

Now that you have finished your action plan, choose one or two people to share it with.

1. What is the situation or relationship that you would like to impact?
2. What are the stumbling blocks you may run into?
3. What is your plan?

Take this time to share with the partner you worked with what you feel God is calling you to do.

Thank you for taking this time to share with your partner what you feel God is calling you to do. Are there any reflections from this experience that you would like to share with the group? *(Give participants time to answer)*.

Closing

We have stepped into the Old Testament understanding of the importance of time. In her time, Esther had the opportunity to save her people from extermination. In his time, Jesus had the power to save all people from sin and its punishment.

We have had time today to think about several things.

1. How do I empty myself so that God can fill me up?
2. What kind of time is this in my life? What am I being called to do?
3. What are my stumbling blocks? How can these obstacles be turned into stepping-stones?
4. What specific actions do I need to take in order to do what God wants me to do with my life at this time?

Thank you for sharing yourself today, for opening your heart to God to fill you, for considering what God has uniquely equipped and empowered you to do. Let's celebrate the decisions that have been made and the new commitments that we will take from this event today.

(A Service of Holy Communion can be added here, beginning with the Prayer of Great Thanksgiving and following the liturgy from *The United Methodist Hymnal*, pp. 13-15.)

Closing Music:
#593 "Here I Am, Lord" * * *
#2163 "He Who Began a Good Work in You" * *

Let's close our time together with prayer.

*Prayer

We thank you, God, for Esther's courage to speak up in behalf of her people. We thank you for Mordecai's refusal to bow down and worship anyone but you. You created all of us with unique gifts, and you summon us to use them—to take risks, to be courageous, to act, to lead.

Forgive us for the times that we have settled for being ordinary. We've stood back and criticized when we could have made a positive contribution. We've been overwhelmed by the size of our problems instead of letting you overwhelm us by making us part of the solutions. You constantly remind us that your power is ours because we are your children. Thank you for sharing yourself with us and allowing us to share ourselves with others during this time we have spent together. Help us to follow through on what we have been empowered to do today. In Christ's name we pray. Amen.

*Benediction

"May you go forth and fulfill your calling, in the name of Christ. May you do it with the courage of Esther!"

Children's Program Suggestions

In the Jewish tradition, Purim (pronounced poorim) is a day of joy in February or March, marked by feasting and merrymaking. *Esther* is read from a scroll in the synagogue. Hearers make noise to blot out the name of Haman with noisemakers called groggers, which make the sound of metallic grinding. Gifts are exchanged, money is given to the poor, Purim plays are presented, and costumes are worn. Purim flags have recently been added to the celebration, with small bells attached that jingle in triumph each time the names of Vashti or Esther are mentioned.

Esther's story can be enjoyed by children in Christian churches in much the way that Purim is celebrated as a Jewish festival. Activities for a children's party or program can include one or more of the following:

Create a scroll of the story of Esther, to be read aloud.

Create flags that children decorate with drawings of Esther. Attach bells that make soft sounds.

Make groggers by creating a shaker out of paper plates folded in half with beans inside, stapled around the edges.

Create masks and/or costumes for the characters in the story.

Make puppets and do a puppet show of the story.

Dressed in costumes or masks, children pantomime the actions while the story is told or read.

Hand out the groggers and flags to the audience and encourage the audience to make noise when Haman's name is mentioned and wave their flags when Vashti or Esther are mentioned.

Uses

- Women's Day Apart: *Guide included.*
- In place of a sermon in any style of worship.
- Mother's Day message.
- Retreat for high school girls or college women.
- Church planning retreat or meeting.
- Children's party or program: *Suggestions included.*

The Revised Common Lectionary
   Year B, Sunday between September 25 and October 1 inclusive: Esther 7:1-6, 9-10, 9:20-22

✱ ✱ ✱

*Congregation invited to stand.
**The Faith We Sing
***The United Methodist Hymnal
****Draw Me Close: 25 Top Vineyard Worship Songs

---

1. Marianne Larned, *Stone Soup For the World* (New York: Three Rivers Press, 2000).
2. Ibid.
3. Ibid.
4. Churches in cities across America have united to assist in caring for homeless people through Room in the Inn. One example is at Nashville, Tennessee. Go to www.chd-nashville.org/room-in-the-inn for information.

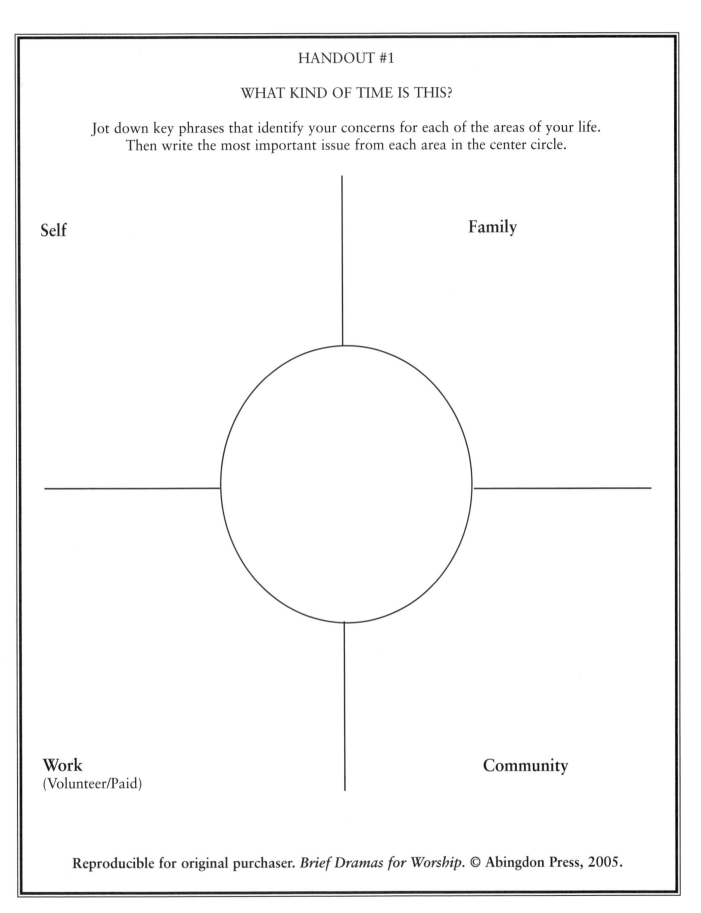

HANDOUT #1

WHAT KIND OF TIME IS THIS?

Jot down key phrases that identify your concerns for each of the areas of your life.
Then write the most important issue from each area in the center circle.

Self

Family

Work
(Volunteer/Paid)

Community

HANDOUT #2
PREPARATION FOR CHANGE

1. SEEING CLEARLY HOW SOMETHING CAN BE BETTER. Develop a clear picture of what it would look like if things were the way God wants them to be. Esther 4:14

2. SEEING THE IMPORTANCE OF MAKING A CHANGE. Examine the consequences of making or not making a change. Esther 4:10-11

3. REALIZING THAT YOU CAN MAKE A DIFFERENCE. Examine how God has uniquely equipped you to institute this situation. Compare Esther 4:4-11 to 5:1-3

4. KNOWING HOW TO DO IT. This involves deciding what action to take and identifying specific support, training, and resources needed to get the job done. Esther 4:15-16

5. SEEKING SUPPORT FROM OTHERS. Who shares your concern and is willing to provide support for you as you make the needed changes? Esther 4:16

HANDOUT #3
STUMBLING BLOCKS

LACK OF CLEAR GOALS

POOR COMMUNICATION

FEAR

LACK OF SUPPORT OF KEY PEOPLE

SATISFACTION WITH THE WAY THINGS ARE

ACTION PLAN

WHAT IS THE SITUATION OR RELATIONSHIP THAT I WOULD LIKE TO IMPACT?

WHAT ARE THE STUMBLING BLOCKS I MAY RUN INTO?

WHAT ARE THE ACTION STEPS THAT I AM GOING TO FOLLOW?

WHAT AM I GOING TO DO TODAY AS A RESULT OF THIS ACTION PLAN?

Suggestions for Use During the Church Year

- **Advent:**
  - ❏ The Bethlehem Child: Children in Poverty

- **Christmas Season:**
  - ❏ Christmas Eve: Eli's Wife: A Husband's Tale Brings Hope for Peace
  - ❏ Watch Night (New Year's Eve): Bathsheba and King Dave: The Bigger the Ego, the Harder the Fall

- **Season of Epiphany:**
  - ❏ Second Sunday in January (Baptism of the Lord Sunday/Congregational Reaffirmation of the Baptismal Covenant): Caroline: A Waitress Receives the Living Water of Acceptance and Hope
  - ❏ Any Sunday during Epiphany (A Service of Healing): Storm-Tossed Family and Dried-Up Hope: Jesus' Power over Storms

- **Season in Lent:**
  - ❏ Ash Wednesday: Bathsheba and King Dave: The Bigger the Ego, the Harder the Fall
  - ❏ Third Sunday in Lent: Caroline: A Waitress Receives the Living Water of Acceptance and Hope
  - ❏ Fourth Sunday in Lent (Heritage Sunday/Conjunction with Membership Class/Women's Sunday): Mary Fletcher: A Young Woman's Faith Leads to Holiness and Reform
  - ❏ Holy Week: Mary: Daring to Hope Again

- **Easter Season:**
  - ❏ Fourth Sunday of Easter (Heritage Sunday/Senior Citizen Sunday): Mary Fletcher: A Young Woman's Faith Leads to Holiness and Reform
  - ❏ Fifth Sunday of Easter: Martha: Prescription for Peace
  - ❏ Seventh Sunday of Easter: Lydia: A Witness to the Power of Christ to Open Hearts, Open Minds, and Open Doors
  - ❏ Mother's Day: Esther: Chosen for Such a Time as This **or** Margaret: A Grieving Mother Yearns for Her Wayward Son

- **Ordinary Time:**
  - ❏ July
    - ■ Mattie May: A Mountain Woman's Tale of a Gracious Plenty (Begin plans for a Mission Festival)
    - ■ Bathsheba and King Dave: The Bigger the Ego, The Harder the Fall (Summer retreat for youth)
    - ■ Esther: Chosen for Such a Time as This (Women's Retreat)

❏ **August**
- Margaret: A Grieving Mother Yearns for Her Wayward Son

❏ **August or September**
- Mattie May: A Mountain Woman's Tale of a Gracious Plenty (Stewardship Drive)

❏ **October**
- Mattie May: A Mountain Woman's Tale of a Gracious Plenty (World Communion Sunday)
- The Bethlehem Child: Children in Poverty (Children's Sabbath)
- Storm-Tossed Family and Dried-Up Hope: Jesus' Power Over Storms (A Service of Healing)

Source List

Please obtain any necessary copyright permissions before using these sources.

MUSIC

***The Faith We Sing*. Nashville: Abingdon Press.

****The United Methodist Hymnal*. Nashville: The United Methodist Publishing House.

*****Draw Me Close: 25 Top Vineyard Worship Songs* 2002 Vineyard Music. Marketed by EMI Christian Music Group. Distributed by Chordant Distribution Group, P.O. Box 5084, Brentwood, Tenn. 37024-5084. Available in printed music and CD.

WOW Worship Yellow 2003 Songbook. Franklin, Tenn.: Brentwood-Benson Music Publishing, Inc., 2003.
• "Oh Lord, You're Beautiful."
Performed by Keith Green on *WOW Worship* Yellow CD.

• "Come Now Is the Time to Worship"
Performed by Phillips, Craig and Dean on *WOW Worship* Yellow CD.

• "I Stand Amazed"
Performed by GlassByrd on *WOW Worship* Yellow CD.

"Love Came Down" performed by Lindell Cooley on *Open Up the Sky*. Hosanna! Music, 2001. Also in *Hosanna! Music Songbook 16*.

"Dive" performed by Steven Curtis Chapman on *Speechless*. Sparrow Records, 1999.

"Give Me a New Heart" written and performed by John Wyrosdick on *My Redeemer Lives* album. Vineyard Music Group, 1996.

"How Beautiful" performed by Twila Paris on *Greatest Hits*. Sparrow/Emd, 2001

"On My Knees" performed by Jaci Velasquez on *Heavenly Place*. Sony, 1996.

TEXT

The New Interpreter's Bible. Vol. II. Nashville: Abingdon Press, 1996.

The United Methodist Book of Worship. Nashville: The United Methodist Publishing House, thirteenth printing 2002. [Calendar of *The Revised Common Lectionary* is listed on pp. 227-237.]

The Revised Common Lectionary. Nashville: Abingdon Press, 1991.

Anti-Slavery Society. Online: www.anti-slaverysociety.addr.com/ckab.htm

Brown, Susan Taylor. *Can I Pray With My Eyes Open*. Winnipeg, Manitoba, Canada: Hyperion Books for Children, 1999.

Edelman, Marian Wright. *Hold My Hands: Prayer for Building a Movement to Leave No Child Behind*. Washington D.C.: Children's Defense Fund, 2001.

Forest, Heather. *Stone Soup*. Little Rock, Ark.: August House Little Folk, 1998.

Kraybill, Ronald S. *Peace Skills: Manual for Community Mediators*. San Francisco: Jossey Bass, Inc., 2001.

Larned, Marianne., ed. *Stone Soup for the World: Life-Changing Stories of Everyday Heroes*. New York: Three Rivers Press, first published 1998, 2002.

Moore, Henry. *The Life of Mrs. Mary Fletcher*. London: J. Kershaw, 1824.

Munsch, Robert. *Love You Forever*. Canada: Firefly Books Ltd., 1999.

NCH Fact Sheet #1 and #2. The National Coalition for the Homeless, September 2002.

Ritual in a New Day: An Invitation. Nashville: Abingdon Press, 1976.

Rogers, Fred. *The World According to Mister Rogers*. New York: Hyperion Books, 2003.

Springer, Jane. *Listen to Us: The World's Working Children*. Toronto, Ontario: Groundwood Books, 1997.

Ware, Corinne. *Saint Benedict on the Freeway: A Rule of Life for the 21st Century*. Nashville: Abingdon Press, 2001.

Williams, Colin W. *John Wesley's Theology Today*. Nashville: Abingdon Press, 1960.

VIDEO

"A Day at the Circus" and "Adventures in Friendship." *Mister Rogers' Neighborhood*. VHS/DVD published by Anchor Bay Entertainment, 2005.

Simon Birch. Hollywood Pictures Company, 1998. Written and directed by Mark Steven Johnson.

The Mission. Warner Communications Company, 1986. Written by Robert Bolt and directed by Roland Joffe.